George W. (George Washington) King

Kolasis Aionios or Future Retribution

George W. (George Washington) King

Kolasis Aionios or Future Retribution

ISBN/EAN: 9783337140816

Printed in Europe, USA, Canada, Australia, Japan

Cover: Foto ©Lupo / pixelio.de

More available books at **www.hansebooks.com**

ΚΌΛΑΣΙΣ ΑΙΏΝΙΟΣ

OR

FUTURE RETRIBUTION

By GEORGE W. KING

Pastor of the Broadway Methodist Episcopal Church, Providence, R. I.

"It is a fearful thing to fall into the hands of the living God."—HEB. x, 31

NEW YORK: HUNT & EATON
CINCINNATI: CRANSTON & STOWE
1892

PREFACE.

WE are persuaded that the *a priori* method of argument is too much used on both sides of this question. When used by the orthodox writer it is a bad example to his opponent, who finds an unlimited occasion for its use. In the present discussion, which we have undertaken to make both thorough and brief, we have appealed to fact, ignoring the *a priori* when in conflict with this, and have thus sought to be strictly scientific in our method. We have not sought novelty for its own sake, but the truth; and where this could be served by the new or the old, we have not hesitated to accept either. Subservient to this aim, we think will be found in treatment and in thought sufficient that is new to justify publication, and make profitable the perusal of the present pages. Definiteness of thought and statement has also been an aim. Vagueness is too much the bane of too much theology, and the present doctrine has not escaped its influence. We have sought to be both specific and exact. There has been no particular attempt at rhetorical effect. This may be legitimate in the treatment of a subject that is well accepted in the Church; but not, from our standpoint, in the scientific investigation and exposition of a doctrine so much in dispute as the present one. It may, however, be proper elsewhere, and we think the preacher will find in our treatment facts and seed-thoughts that may be properly elaborated in his public ministrations. Courtesy has been our rule toward opponents; but also loyalty to truth and fact.

Our line of treatment, without being distinctly specified, has been *Fact, Nature*, and *Reason;* the first embracing chapters i–v; the second, chapters vi and vii; the eighth chapter, in which we occupy a quite independent position, comprehending our entire discussion of the Reason, which might easily have been expanded into several but for our law of brevity.

Among the works read and consulted in the immediate preparation of this book are the following: Thayer's *Greek-English Lexicon of the New Testament;* Edersheim's *Life and Times of the Messiah* (appendix xix); Vincent's *Word Studies in the New Testament;* Shedd's *Dogmatic Theology* (vol. ii, pp. 667–754); Müller's

Christian Doctrine of Sin; Dorner's *System of Christian Doctrine* (vol. iv, pp. 127-132 and 373-434. Also, *Dorner on the Future State,* Smyth); *Christian Dogmatics,* Martensen; *Future Retribution,* C. A. Row; *Future Probation Examined,* William DeLoss Love; *Biblical Eschatology,* Hovey; *Is there Salvation After Death?* E. D. Morris; *Spirits in Prison,* Plumptre; *Salvator Mundi,* Cox; *Restitution of All Things,* Jukes; *Life in Christ,* White; *Extinction of Evil,* Petavel; *What is of Faith as to Everlasting Punishment?* Pusey; *Eternal Hope* and *Mercy and Judgment,* Farrar; *Is "Eternal" Punishment Endless?* Whiton; etc. And while acknowledging our indebtedness to all of these sources for suggestion and facts, we have, for the most part, pursued an independent course in that we have at least sought to verify for ourselves.

Hoping the book may serve a useful purpose, we commit it to the candid attention of those to whom it shall come, and in the interest of the truth we have sought to defend and expound.

G. W. K.

PROVIDENCE, R. I., *March* 25, 1891.

CONTENTS.

CHAPTER I.
The Eternity of Punishment.................. 9

CHAPTER II.
Objections and Arguments of Restorationists.. 53

CHAPTER III.
New Testament Terminology Respecting Future Retribution........................ 115

CHAPTER IV.
The Ground of Future Endless Retribution; Or, For What the Wicked are Punished Eternally............................ 141

CHAPTER V.
The Number of the Lost..................... 193

CHAPTER VI.
The Nature of Future Punishment.......... 209

CHAPTER VII.
The Doctrine of Annihilation.............. 217

CHAPTER VIII.
The Reason or Law of Necessity in Future Punishment................................ 247

"To the law and to the testimony: if they speak not according to this word, it is because there is no light in them."—Isa. viii, 20.

ΚΌΛΑΣΙΣ ΑΊΏΝΙΟΣ;

OR,

FUTURE RETRIBUTION.

CHAPTER I.

The Eternity of Punishment.

THE fact of future retribution simply and as such is not now to be considered, since all writers who accept the Bible as a divine revelation are agreed as to its reality.* The question before us is the question of duration: Is there endless future punishment of the wicked? At this point there is much dispute, and its answer furnishes the chief ground of interest for the

---

*It is seldom in our day that we find a writer, as Dr. W. E. Manley in the *Arena* for April, 1890, advocating the idea that the punishment of men is limited to this life. We once heard a Universalist minister, in the city of Baltimore, in a sermon in response to a lecture by Joseph Cook, in which Mr. Cook spoke of the eternal punishment of Aaron Burr and men like him, say: "After Aaron Burr has been in hell ten thousand years, perhaps he will be ready for heaven," or words to that effect. Practically, the opinion of writers on the subject is unanimous in favor of some punishment after death.

whole subject. We come, therefore, immediately to it, and attempt its settlement.

Of course, the answer to our inquiry must be scriptural.* No other answer is adequate or proper. Philosophy cannot answer it, for it is outside the realm of philosophy. It is a question of fact, and one which, if it is to be known at all, must be learned from the divine declarations. We proceed, therefore, to the biblical or exegetical consideration of the doctrine. Does the Bible teach the endless future punishment of the wicked?

Making our appeal alone to the Scriptures, we believe one, and only one, answer is possible. It is the affirmative. This we proceed to prove.

1. The most direct biblical support of the doctrine is Matt. xxv, 46: "And these shall go away into eternal punishment: but the righteous into eternal life" (R. V.).

Except question were raised as to the natural and obvious import of this text it might be left

---

* We say "of course," not because every writer follows this plan properly or faithfully, but because however much some ignore it in practice, all admit the validity of it as a principle of procedure. An exception, however, to this statement is found in the case of those who, with Dorner, appeal for doctrine to the Scriptures and to "faith," or to the Scriptures and the so-called "Christian Consciousness." But we have nothing to do with this doctrine in this place.

to stand as it is, as God's warning against sin, without comment; but since it is declared in certain quarters not to be so alarming as it appears to the reader of the common English Bible, it becomes necessary to direct attention to what the language involves.

Perhaps even the average layman has already become familiar with the fact that the words "everlasting" and "eternal" in the Authorized Version are translations of the same word (αἰώνιος) in the original. This is made evident in the Revised Version by the substitution of the word "eternal" for "everlasting" in the first clause of the verse as found in the Authorized. The important fact learned here is that the duration expressed in the one case must be expressed also in the other; that is, whatever the duration of the future life of the righteous, that also, so far as this text is concerned in its express teaching, must be the duration of the punishment of the wicked. If the one is eternal in the sense of endlessness, so also is the other.*

---

* Dr. Farrar tries to minify the force of this simple but impregnable argument by stigmatizing it as "time-worn," as though, other things being equal, this did not strengthen rather than weaken it. Its manifest fairness will remain despite such unscientific slurs.

On the other hand, Canon Row, in his *Future Retribution*, admits the force of the parallel, and limiting the sense of αἰώνιος in the one case, he limits it also in the other. According

2. Matt. xii, 31, 32: "Therefore I say unto you, Every sin and blasphemy shall be forgiven to him, the future endless life of the righteous is not revealed, but is derived from considerations of the divine love and mercy. He says (pp. 266, 267): "I fully admit that the word αἰώνιος, when united with ζωή, life, must have the same meaning as it bears when it is in the same sentence united with the words κόλασις or πῦρ. But there is this difference between the two cases. When the æon, or æons, denoted by the word αἰώνιος, are coming to a close, all holy beings will still be able to look up to Him who is, and who was, and who is to come, the Almighty, as the unchangeable father of mercies and the God of all comfort, and as in his essential being, love; and their 'abiding in love,' causing them to abide in God and God in them, affords the strongest ground for trust that their life with God will never end. Full well, therefore, may they be satisfied during the æons of the future with living in that state of hope and trust in God in which the saints of the Old Testament lived and died, though its pages contain no express revelation of a life to come. Yet, as we have seen, not a few of the most enlightened saints of that dispensation entertained the firmest faith, notwithstanding the clouds and darkness with which God's present providences were enshrouded, that it would be finally well with those who loved God, and who lived in obedience to his laws. Why, then, should not the inheritor of the perfected kingdom of God be satisfied with the same assurance as supported his Jewish brother during the age in which he lived, that God, who is unchangeable in his perfections, will never desert them that love him throughout all the ages of the future, when, to use the words of the apostle, 'God will be all in all?' This is an assurance on which we may rely with far more fullness of conviction than on a word which varies so greatly in meaning as the word αἰώνιος, 'eternal.'"

Such teaching, while that only which is logically tenable from the denial that future endless punishment is taught in the text, is an example of the straits to which those who deny this doctrine are frequently driven.

unto men; but the blasphemy against the Spirit shall not be forgiven. And whosoever shall speak a word against the Son of man, it shall be forgiven him; but whosoever shall speak against the Holy Spirit, it shall not be forgiven him, neither in this world [marg., "age"], nor in that which is to come."

The parallel passage in Mark is as follows: "Verily I say unto you, All their sins shall be forgiven unto the sons of men, and their blasphemies wherewith soever they shall blaspheme: but whosoever shall blaspheme against the Holy Spirit hath never forgiveness, but is guilty of an eternal sin: because they said, He hath an unclean spirit" (chap. iii, 28–30. Compare 1 John v, 16. I do not take it that Heb. vi, 4–8; x, 26–29, is the same sin.)

Evidently these two passages, being parallel accounts of the same conversation of our Lord, have the same meaning, and cast light upon each other. We have in them two negative statements of the most conclusive character. In Mark the Greek is οὐκ ἔχει ἄφεσιν εἰς τὸν αἰῶνα, ἀλλὰ ἔνοχός ἐσται αἰωνίου ἁμαρτήματος. Says an able writer in the *Bibliotheca Sacra* for January, 1889: "However plausibly it may be urged that αἰώνιος does not, in the Scripture references to a future life, mean 'everlasting,' and that εἰς τοὺς αἰῶνας does not really mean 'forever,' no scholar will undertake to deny that οὐ—εἰς τοὺς αἰῶνας is biblical Greek for an English emphatic, unqualified *never*. The phrase has various forms (εἰς τὸν αἰῶνα, εἰς τοὺς αἰῶνας, ἕως αἰῶνος, etc.), but they are all combinations of the noun αἰών with some preposition and with a foregoing negative. It always, so far as I have noted, both in the Septuagint and in the New Testament, answers either to the English 'not—forever,' or to 'never.' In the former case it denies permanence or future perpetuity to that which already exists or is conceived as existing; for example, Job vii, 16, οὐ γὰρ εἰς τὸν αἰῶνα ζήσομαι, 'for I shall not live forever;' Psa. ciii, 9, οὐκ εἰς τέλος ὀργισθήσεται, οὐδὲ εἰς τὸν αἰῶνα μηνιεῖ, 'He will not be always angry, neither will he be wrathful forever.' But in the majority of instances in biblical Greek it is equivalent to *never*, when used not with reference to the *past* (for example, John vii, 46, οὐδέποτε ἐλάλησεν οὕτως ἄνθρωπος, 'Never man so spake'), nor to the *present* (for example, 1 Cor. xiii, 8, ἡ ἀγάπη οὐδέποτε πίπτει, 'Love never faileth'), but to the *future*, as in John iv, 14, 'But whosoever drinketh,' etc., 'shall never thirst' (οὐ μὴ διψήσει εἰς τὸν αἰῶνα); 1 Cor. viii, 13, 'Wherefore if meat maketh my brother to stumble, I will never eat flesh' (R. V., 'eat no flesh for evermore;' A. V., 'eat no flesh while the world standeth'). It is further to be observed that while there are various other Greek words and phrases which answer to our emphatic future *never*, this of which we are speaking is one of the most frequent in the New Testament. In order to ascertain its meaning in Hellenistic Greek it is not necessary to fix the various significations of the term αἰών, considered simply as a substantive; the phrase is one concerning which no doubt, at least in the majority of passages, can be raised. Now this is the term which we find in that impressive warning of our Saviour to his antagonists recorded in Mark iii, 29, 'But whosoever shall blaspheme against the Holy Spirit hath never forgiveness, but is guilty of an eternal sin' (οὐκ ἔχει ἄφεσιν εἰς τὸν αἰῶνα, ἀλλὰ ἔνοχός ἐστιν αἰωνίου ἁμαρτήματος). In this one passage, at least, we are compelled to recognize an unequivocal, emphatic, absolute *never*."

Likewise, whatever the phrase οὔτε ἐν τούτῳ τῷ αἰῶνι οὔτε ἐν τῷ μέλλοντι ("neither in this world, nor in that which is to come") in Matthew may signify, in the way of inference, as to the possible restoration in another life of those who do *not* commit this sin, clearly for it there will be no forgiveness.*

3. Rev. xx, 10-15 : " And the devil that deceived them was cast into the lake of fire and brimstone, where are also the beast and the false prophet ; and they shall be tormented day and night for ever and ever.

" And I saw a great white throne, and him that sat upon it, from whose face the earth and the heaven fled away ; and there was found no place for them. And I saw the dead, the great and the small, standing before the throne ; and books

---

* Some (among them Dorner) try to evade the force of this argument by suggesting that, while the sin against the Holy Ghost hath never *forgiveness*, yet the penalty may come to an end, and restoration even in this case take place. Well might it be asked, in view of interpretations of this character frequently found in the writings of Universalists, "whether there is any way, in which Almighty God *could* have expressed it [the eternity of punishment], which they would have accepted as meaning it." Besides, in this case some would be saved without the atonement. Their salvation would be by paying the penalty, not through Christ. Exegesis that is put to such shifts may well be regarded unsound.

Dorner suggests, also, that "the passages concerning the sin against the Holy Ghost say nothing of definite persons who have committed this sin. Of themselves, therefore, they leave the question unanswered, what men, and whether any men, reach this final goal of criminality, which is set before the eyes as a warning. Just so the Revelation of John does not say who, or that a man will be cast into the lake of fire ; the hypothetical form is rather chosen : 'If one is not inscribed in the book of

were opened: and another book was opened, which is the book of life: and the dead were judged out of the things which were written in the books, according to their works. And the sea gave up the dead which were in it; and death and Hades gave up the dead which were in them: and they were judged every man according to their works. And death and Hades were cast into the lake of fire. This is the second death, even the lake of fire. And if any was not found written in the book of life, he was cast into the lake of fire." (Compare Rev. xiv, 9-11; xix, 20; xxi, 8.)

Whatever there may be that is figurative in

life,' 'if one worships the beast, he shall drink the cup of wrath,' all which affirms nothing of persons, but of the principle." But this, likewise, is a pure evasion of the solemn teaching contained in these passages of Scripture.

Since writing the last paragraph of this note we have met still another device, equally untenable, by which the fearful import of this passage is sought to be avoided. It seeks to show that "deliverance" from this sin may possibly be had through *repentance* (*Unto the Uttermost*, James M. Campbell, p. 125). We would ask: (1) Is there deliverance from any sin except through repentance? And if not, wherein, on this supposition, lies the difference between the sin against the Holy Ghost and the sin against the "Son of man?" (2) Is this compatible with the words "it shall not be forgiven him [not 'so long as he continues in an unyielding, unrepentant state,' but plainly], neither in this world, nor in that which is to come?" (3) What is "deliverance" from this sin without *forgiveness*, which shall never be exercised?

these verses, if they mean any thing the following points are clear: (1) The devil is to be cast into the lake of fire, and his punishment is to last "for ever and ever." (2) After the resurrection the dead are to be judged "according to their works." (3) Those whose names are not found written in the book of life are to be cast into the lake of fire.

Taken in connection with Matt. xxv, 31–46, the evidence for the endlessness of the punishment of the wicked furnished here becomes as convincing as language can very well make it.*

4. Mark ix, 43–48: "And if thy hand cause thee to stumble, cut it off: it is good for thee to enter into life maimed, rather than having thy two hands to go into hell, into the unquenchable fire. And if thy foot cause thee to stumble, cut it off: it is good for thee to enter into life

---

* If the reader will carefully compare the two passages he will be impressed with the following points of agreement and parallel: 1. Both concern the general judgment. 2. The resurrection is in both passages represented as having taken place. 3. Those whose names were not found written in the book of life (the "goats" of Matthew) were cast into the lake of fire prepared for the devil and his angels (Matt., verse 41; Rev., verses 10, 15). 4. The two phrases, βασανισθήσονται . . . εἰς τοὺς αἰῶνας τῶν αἰώνων (Rev., verse 10) and κόλασιν αἰώνιον (Matt., verse 46), seem to be identical in signification. The force of this last parallel will be felt in connection with the general parallel of the entire passages.

THE ETERNITY OF PUNISHMENT. 19

halt, rather than having thy two feet to be cast into hell. And if thine eye cause thee to stumble, cast it out : it is good for thee to enter into the kingdom of God with one eye, rather than having two eyes to be cast into hell ; where their worm dieth not, and the fire is not quenched." (Compare Matt. iii, 12 ; v, 29, 30; xviii, 8, 9.)

In connection with this passage two points of interest demand brief attention : (1) The first is concerning the word " hell." The alternate reading in the margin of the Revised Version is " Gehenna." This word (γέεννα) comes from the Hebrew גֵּי הִנֹּם (gē hinnom), literally, " valley of Hinnom." (Some would translate "valley of lamentation.") The valley of Hinnom, also called תֹּפֶת (" Topheth "), once a beautiful valley, became the place of the worship of the fire-god Molech, to whom human sacrifices were offered. After Josiah " defiled " the place, " that no man might make his son or his daughter to pass through the fire to Molech," it became the place where the bodies of criminals, the carcasses of animals, and all manner of filth were cast. Here, literally, the worm never died, and to prevent pestilence a fire was kept burning perpetually. From these facts the place became the symbol of the place of future punishment, the latter receiving the name of the former. And so in the time of Christ Gehenna was every-where among the Jews understood to signify the place of torment in Sheol, or Hades. (See *Word Studies in the New Testament*, Marvin R. Vincent, vol. i, page 40, and *Greek-English Lexicon of the New Testament*, Thayer, page 111.) (2) In verse 43 is the expression "unquenchable fire" (τὸ πῦρ τὸ ἄσβεστον); in verse 48, "and the fire is not quenched" (καὶ τὸ πῦρ οὐ σβέννυται). In the parallel account in Matt. xviii, 8, 9, the expression is τὸ πῦρ τὸ αἰώνιον, "the eternal fire." These expressions, remembered in connection with other teachings of Christ, furnish terrible proof of the reality of the doctrine we are considering.

It avails nothing to say that they do not "necessarily" teach endless suffering. Alone they may not be thought sufficient to prove the doctrine, but in the light of other sayings of Christ they have no doubtful meaning.

5. Matt. xxvi, 24: "The Son of man goeth, even as it is written of him: but woe unto that man through whom the Son of man is betrayed! good were it for that man if he had not been born."

This passage never could have been uttered by Christ with the knowledge in this case of final restoration; for if Judas is to be saved some time in the future, no matter how far distant the day may be, he will still have an eternity of blessedness reserved for him, and in view of this, despite the long season of punishment, it could only be said: "It was good for him that he was born." No amount of *temporal* punishment can outweigh the "good" of *eternal* life.*

6. Jude 5–16: "Now I desire to put you in remembrance, though ye know all things once for all, how that the Lord, having saved a people out of the land of Egypt, afterward destroyed them that believed not. And angels which kept not their own principality, but left their proper habitation, he hath kept in everlasting bonds under darkness unto the judgment of the great day. Even as Sodom and Gomorrah, and the cities about them, having in like manner with these given themselves over to fornication, and gone after strange flesh, are set forth as an example, suffering the punishment of eternal fire. Yet in like manner these also in their dreamings defile the flesh, and set at naught dominion, and rail at dignities. But Michael the archangel, when

---

* The argument here is only an inference, we know, but it is nevertheless very strong. Dorner calls it the "strongest" on the orthodox side.

contending with the devil he disputed about the body of Moses, durst not bring against him a railing judgment, but said, The Lord rebuke thee. But these rail at whatsoever things they know not: and what they understand naturally, like the creatures without reason, in these things are they destroyed. Woe unto them! for they went in the way of Cain, and ran riotously in the error of Baalam for hire, and perished in the gainsaying of Korah. These are they who are hidden rocks in your love-feasts when they feast with you, shepherds that without fear feed themselves; clouds without water, carried along by winds; autumn trees without fruit, twice dead, plucked up by the roots; wild waves of the sea, foaming out their own shame; wandering stars, for whom the blackness of darkness hath been reserved forever. And to these also Enoch, the seventh from Adam, prophesied, saying, Behold, the Lord came with ten thousands of his holy ones, to execute judgment upon all, and to convict all the ungodly of all their works of ungodliness which they have ungodly wrought, and of all the hard things which ungodly sinners have spoken against him. These are murmurers, complainers, walking after their lusts (and their mouth speaketh great swelling words), showing respect of persons for the sake of advantage." (Compare 2 Pet. ii.)

In this passage several things are given: (1) The Israelites who believed not, and the angels "which kept not their own principality," and the inhabitants of the cities of the plain are exhibited as examples of suffering punishment for those of whom Jude is speaking. (2) Certain persons in the early Church are threatened with like punishment. (3) The Israelites were "destroyed" (ἀπώλεσεν); the angels "hath he kept in everlasting (ἀιδίοις) bonds under darkness unto the judgment of the great day;" Sodom and the neighboring cities " are set forth as an example, suffering the punishment of eternal fire " (πυρὸς αἰωνίου). The margin of the Revised Version has for the last, " as an example of eternal fire suffering punishment." For the wicked ones of whom Jude writes has been reserved the " blackness of darkness " " forever " (εἰς αἰῶνα).

Does Jude mean to teach the same punishment in all these cases under different language? Is the " destruction " of the Israelites, and the " reservation " of the angels, and the " suffering " of the Sodomites, and the " blackness of darkness forever " reserved for those of whom he writes, the same punishment in each case? Our answer to this cannot be dogmatic. The case of the cities of the plain is made uncertain by the alternate reading. Perhaps, following the marginal reading, the temporal destruction of these cities is referred to as illustrative only of future punishment. Following the text, it might seem that their eternal punishment is involved. In the case of the Israelites who believed not, we suppose their temporal destruction (Num. xiv, especially verses 11, 29, 32) is referred to. Whether or not more is involved in this case also we do not undertake to say. As to the angels, no doubt can be entertained as to the reference. They are in some sense bound, and in this condition await the judgment. As to their fate at and after the judgment, other Scriptures tell us (Rev. xx, 10; Matt. xxv, 41). The fate of the last class can be no other than that spoken of elsewhere concerning the wicked; and when it is thus associated with the end of the lost angels,* the meaning can only be the same as that taught elsewhere in the New Testament. This we have seen, and will further see, is everlasting punishment.

---

* We call attention again to the fact that the end of devils and wicked men is the same in the New Testament. (Compare Rev. xx, 10, 15, with Matt. xxv, 41.)

7. There is a passage that is frequently quoted to prove the final restoration of the lost, but that is so manifestly in favor of the doctrine of eternal punishment that we place it here among the proofs of the doctrine. It will be considered more fully, however, when we come to notice the arguments advanced in favor of Universalism. The passage we refer to is 1 Cor. xv, 24-26:

"Then cometh the end, when he shall deliver up the kingdom to God, even the Father; when he shall have abolished all rule and all authority and power. For he must reign, till he hath put all his enemies under his feet. The last enemy that shall be abolished is death."

The points to be noted are: (1) The end of the mediatorial reign of Christ follows the destruction of the "last enemy," and (2) the last enemy to be abolished is *physical* death at and by the resurrection. Now, remember in connection with this, that the coming (parousia) of Christ and the resurrection are *followed* by the judgment (Matt. xxv, 31; Rev. xx, 12-14; xxii, 10-12), and that, according to Matt. xxv, 31-46, and other Scriptures, the "æonian punishment" is pronounced *after* the "last enemy," death, has been abolished, and the passage furnishes an argument for eternal punishment that is unanswerable.

We urge these facts as worthy all consideration. If the "last enemy" to be abolished is physical death, and the κόλασις αἰώνιος of Matthew *follows* this destruction, then the thought of the "second death" being abolished is absolutely excluded. The *last* enemy is abolished in the resurrection, and before the κόλασις αἰώνιος, or ὁ θάνατος ὁ δεύτερός, is awarded. (Compare also John v, 28, 29.)

8. Another proof of the endlessness of future punishment is furnished in those passages of Scripture which reveal what Dr. Tayler Lewis appropriately calls the "aspect of finality." In Lange's *Commentary on Ecclesiastes* he says: "It may be thought that this view of עוֹלָם and αἰών as having plurals, and therefore not in themselves denoting absolute endlessness, or infinity of time, must weaken the force of certain passages in the New Testament, especially of that most solemn sentence, Matt. xxv, 46. This, however, comes from a wrong view of what constitutes the real power of the impressive language there employed. The preacher, in contending with the Universalist, or Restorationist, would commit an error, and, it may be, suffer a

failure in his argument should he lay the whole stress of it on the etymological or historical significance of the words, αἰών, αἰώνιος, and attempt to prove that, of themselves, they necessarily carry the meaning of endless duration. There is another method by which the conclusion is reached in a much more impressive and cavil-silencing manner. It is by insisting on that dread aspect of *finality* that appears not in single words merely, but in the power and vividness of the language taken as a whole" (page 48).

Some of the passages that have this "dread aspect" are the following:

"Let both grow together until the harvest: and in the time of the harvest I will say to the reapers, Gather up first the tares, and bind them in bundles to burn them: but gather the wheat into my barn" (Matt. xiii, 30).

"Again, the kingdom of heaven is like unto a net, that was cast into the sea, and gathered of every kind: which, when it was filled, they drew up on the beach; and they sat down, and gathered the good into vessels, but the bad they cast away. So shall it be in the end of the world: the angels shall come forth, and sever the wicked from among the righteous, and shall cast them into the furnace of fire: there shall be the weeping and gnashing of teeth" (Matt. xiii, 47–50).

"But when the king came in to behold the guests, he saw there a man which had not on a wedding-garment: and he saith unto him, Friend, how camest thou in hither not having a wedding-garment? And he was speechless. Then the king said to the servants, Bind him hand and foot, and cast him out into the outer darkness; there shall be the weeping and gnashing of teeth" (Matt. xxii, 11–13).

"Then shall the kingdom of heaven be likened unto ten virgins, which took their lamps, and went forth to meet the bridegroom. And five of them were foolish, and five were wise. For the foolish, when they took their lamps, took no oil with them: but the wise took oil in their vessels with their lamps. Now while the bridegroom tarried, they all slumbered and slept. But at midnight there is a cry, Behold, the bridegroom! Come ye forth to meet him. Then all those virgins arose, and trimmed their lamps. And the foolish said unto the wise, Give us of your oil; for our lamps are going out. But the wise answered, saying, Peradventure there will not be enough for us and you: go ye rather to them that sell, and buy for yourselves. And while they went away to buy, the bridegroom came; and they that were ready went in with him to the marriage feast: and the door was shut. Afterward come also the other virgins, saying, Lord, Lord, open to us. But he answered and said, Verily I say unto you, I know you not. Watch therefore, for ye know not the day nor the hour" (Matt. xxv, 1-13).*

" For it is as when a man, going into another country, called his own servants, and delivered

---

* An interesting piece of "wriggling," to use one of Mr. Darwin's terms, of the exegetical type, is given in remarks on this parable by C. A. Row (*Future Retribution*). He comments thus: " The virgins who came prepared with a sufficient supply of oil for their lamps enter at once with the bridegroom into the marriage feast, on which the door is shut. Afterward the five foolish ones, *having obtained the necessary supply of oil*, pray that the door might be opened to give them admittance, but the bridegroom replies that he knows them not. The moral of the parable is drawn by our Lord himself: ' Watch, therefore, for ye know not the day nor the hour.' Nothing is said respecting the subsequent fate of the foolish virgins, who are described as returning after they had procured the necessary supply of oil, except that, notwithstanding their earnest entreaties, they were excluded from the marriage feast. The advice given them to purchase the needful oil, and the fact that they succeeded in doing so, proves that it is impossible to erect a dogma on the mere imagery of a parable " (pages 260, 261). It might be permissible, following this eminent example, to suggest that perhaps the virgins went into the marriage feast *after it was over!* Exegesis of this type is no doubt edifying to a certain class of writers.

unto them his goods. And unto one he gave five talents, to another two, to another one ; to each according to his several ability; and he went on his journey. Straightway he that received the five talents went and traded with them, and made other five talents. In like manner he also that received the two gained other two. But he that received the one went away and digged in the earth, and hid his lord's money. Now after a long time the lord of those servants cometh, and maketh a reckoning with them. And he that received the five talents came and brought other five talents, saying, Lord, thou deliveredst unto me five talents : lo, I have gained other five talents. His lord said unto him, Well done, good and faithful servant : thou hast been faithful over a few things, I will set thee over many things : enter thou into the joy of thy lord. And he also that received the two talents came and said, Lord, thou deliveredst unto me two talents : lo, I have gained other two talents. His lord said unto him, Well done, good and faithful servant ; thou hast been faithful over a few things, I will set thee over many things : enter thou into the joy of thy lord. And he also that had received the one talent came and said, Lord, I knew thee that thou art a hard man, reaping where thou didst not sow, and gathering where thou didst not scatter: and I was afraid, and went away and hid thy talent in the earth: lo, thou hast thine own. But his lord answered and said unto him, Thou wicked and slothful servant, thou knewest that I reap where I sowed not, and gather where I did not scatter; thou oughtest therefore to have put my money to the bankers, and at my coming I should have received back mine own with interest. Take ye away therefore the talent from him, and give it unto him that hath the ten talents. For unto every one that hath shall be given, and he shall have abundance: but from him that hath not, even that which he hath shall be taken away. And cast ye out the unprofitable servant into the outer darkness: there shall be the weeping and gnashing of teeth" (Matt. xxv, 14-30).

"For what doth it profit a man, to gain the whole world, and forfeit his life? For what should a man give in exchange for his life? (Mark viii, 36, 37).

"And beside all this, between us and you there is a great gulf fixed, that they which would pass from hence to you may not be able, and that none may cross over from thence to us" (Luke xvi, 26).

"He said therefore again unto them, I go away, and ye shall seek me, and shall die in your sin: whither I go, ye cannot come" (John viii, 21).

And verse 24: "I said therefore unto you, that ye shall die in your sins: for except ye believe that I am he, ye shall die in your sins."

"For the land which hath drunk the rain that cometh oft upon it, and bringeth forth herbs meet for them for whose sake it is also tilled, receiveth blessing from God: but if it beareth thorns and thistles, it is rejected and nigh unto a curse; whose end is to be burned" (Heb. vi, 7, 8).

"For if we sin willfully after that we have received the knowledge of the truth, there remaineth no more a sacrifice for sins, but a certain fearful expectation of judgment, and a fierceness of fire which shall devour the adversaries" (Heb. x, 26, 27).

In view of all such passages, is it not surprising that some will persist in reading into the Scriptures the delusive hope of final restoration?*

---

*This argument Whiton (*Is Eternal Punishment Endless?* p. 33), thinks is the "strongest apparent implication of the endlessness of future punishment." He says further: "All such passages readily favor the doctrine of the endlessness of that state to which they refer," and saves himself from the positive doctrine by concluding: "The endlessness of future punishment is *not the only theory that will agree with the language of despair* which the texts now before us employ" (p. 34).

9. The doctrine we are considering is still further proved by those passages of Scripture which promise certain final blessings to the righteous only. For example, the "righteous" are to go into "eternal life" (Matt. xxv, 46). Now, if the wicked are to be finally restored, after an indefinite æonian punishment, they, too, will at some time go into æonian life. But is not this excluded by the very designation of the righteous as the inheritors of this privilege? Again, he that "overcometh" is to "eat of the tree of life" (Rev. ii, 7). Shall we contradict the Scriptures and say whether or not men overcome they shall finally have right to the tree of life? Again, to the overcomer is the promise that his name shall not be blotted "out of the book of life" (Rev. iii, 5). Is it not a fair inference that those who do not overcome *shall* have their names blotted out? Where is the right to assert that they shall again be inserted after ages of punishment? Once more, to the persecuted followers of our Lord is the exhortation with promise, "Be thou faithful unto death, and I will give thee the crown of life" (Rev. ii, 10). Are the unfaithful also, at some time, to wear the "crown of life?"

Such passages of Scripture, with their exclusive nature, fully warrant the inference we draw from them. They are clear cases of the law in logic known as the "exclusive" proposition. To say, "Some men are honest," involves the inference that some are not honest. So when the Scriptures designate a certain class as subjects of the divine promises and rewards, by necessary inference the opposite class is excluded from the same privileges. (Examine also John iii, 15, 16; iv, 13, 14; vi, 47, 54-58, etc.)

10. Another proof of the everlastingness of the wicked's doom is furnished in those Scriptures which are by some used to teach the doctrine of annihilation. Concerning this doctrine we have something to say further on (chap. vii). For the present we simply affirm that all such passages preclude the idea of final restoration. We give a few examples:

"For if ye live after the flesh, ye shall die" ($\mu\acute{\epsilon}\lambda\lambda\epsilon\tau\epsilon$ $\mathring{\alpha}\pi o\theta\nu\acute{\eta}\sigma\kappa\epsilon\iota\nu$) (Rom. viii, 13). "The wages of sin is death" ($\theta\acute{\alpha}\nu\alpha\tau o\varsigma$) (Rom. vi, 23). "But rather fear him which is able to destroy ($\mathring{\alpha}\pi o\lambda\acute{\epsilon}\sigma\alpha\iota$) both soul and body in hell" [marg., "Gehenna"] (Matt. x, 28). "For wide is the gate, and broad is the way, that leadeth to destruction ($\epsilon i\varsigma$ $\tau\grave{\eta}\nu$ $\mathring{\alpha}\pi\acute{\omega}\lambda\epsilon\iota\alpha\nu$) (Matt. vii, 13). "Who shall suffer punishment, even eternal destruction (ὄλεθρον αἰώνιον) from the face of the Lord and from the glory of his might." (2 Thess. i, 9). "For he that soweth unto his own flesh shall of the flesh reap corruption (φθοράν); but he that soweth unto the spirit shall of the spirit reap eternal life" (Gal. vi, 8).

On this subject Edward White, who himself teaches the doctrine of annihilation, says: "Surely these are not the words (ἀπώλεια, θάνατος, etc.) which would naturally occur to a writer desiring to convey the idea of universal salvation." Again: "As a theory to be established by criticism, Universalism is based on special pleading; while as a delusive prospect to be set before mankind it is likely, as recent American experience has shown, to ruin innumerable souls, who will neglect the 'day' of salvation for the 'fool's to-morrow,' which never arrives" (*Life in Christ*, pp. 446, 448). Also, another writer, who teaches the doctrine of annihilation, although from a different stand-point from that of Mr. White, says: "The Universalist endeavors to evade this [the writer's conclusion of annihilation] by affirming that when the Scriptures threaten the finally impenitent with destruction, or some kindred term, the thing intended is the destruction of the sin, but the recovery of the sinner." He thinks the principle of interpretation which assigns to such terms this construction "non-natural," and says: "Surely it is a mode of dealing with language which no one would adopt, unless compelled by the exigencies of a theory" (C. A. Row, *ut supra*, pp. 386, 387).

We concur with these writers thus far, and affirm that these passages utterly preclude the idea of final universal restoration.

11. Again, we find proof of the doctrine in the many passages which assert an *unqualified negative* in relation to the lot of the wicked. This appears in several of the passages already given; but we repeat one or two here and add others in order to give the proper emphasis to this important thought. "But whosoever shall speak against the Holy Spirit, it shall not be forgiven him" (Matt. xii, 32). "Ye shall seek me, and shall die in your sin: whither I go, ye cannot come" (John viii, 21). Other Scriptures that have not been given are: "For I say unto you, that none of those men which were bidden shall taste of my supper" (Luke xiv, 24), and "He that believeth on the Son hath eternal life; but he that obeyeth [marg., 'believeth'] not the Son

shall not see life, but the wrath of God abideth on him" (John iii, 36).

All such passages unqualifiedly preclude the hope of life for those included in their intent.

12. Another proof is given in the fact that the duration of the future punishment of the wicked is expressed in the same terms as the duration of the life of the righteous, and in the same phrases as are used concerning the Almighty. This is seen not only in the use of the single adjective αἰώνιος as above given (Matt. xxv, 46), but in such phrases as εἰς αἰῶνα, εἰς τοὺς αἰῶνας τῶν αἰώνων. Examples are as follows: "He that eateth this bread shall live forever" (εἰς τὸν αἰῶνα) (John vi, 58). "To whom be the glory for ever and ever" (εἰς τοὺς αἰῶνας τῶν αἰώνων) (Gal. i, 5). "Now unto the king eternal (τῶν αἰώνων), incorruptible, invisible, the only God, be honor and glory for ever and ever" (εἰς τοὺς αἰῶνας τῶν αἰώνων) (1 Tim. i, 17). "For whom the blackness of darkness hath been reserved forever" (εἰς αἰῶνα) (Jude 13). "To him be the glory and the dominion for ever and ever" (εἰς τοὺς αἰῶνας τῶν αἰώνων) (Rev. i, 6). "And I was dead, and behold, I am alive for evermore" (εἰς τοὺς αἰῶνας τῶν αἰώνων) (*ibid.*, verse 18). "Unto him that sitteth on the throne, and unto

the Lamb, be the blessing, and the honor, and the glory, and the dominion, for ever and ever" (εἰς τοὺς αἰῶνας τῶν αἰώνων) (*ibid.*, v, 13). "And the devil that deceived them was cast into the lake of fire and brimstone, where are also the beast and the false prophet; and they shall be tormented day and night for ever and ever" (εἰς τοὺς αἰῶνας τῶν αἰώνων) (*ibid.*, xx, 10). Language could not more plainly declare the doctrine we teach.

13. The disproof of universal restoration, and thus indirectly the proof of eternal punishment, may be further shown by the disproof of the assertion, so often made, that the future punishment of the New Testament is represented as remedial. It is nowhere referred to as such, but the reverse.

We mention this point simply in this place, and reserve the refutation of the pleasing error for a subsequent chapter.

14. Another argument in favor of the doctrine of endless punishment is found in the fact that the life of man is divided, according to the New Testament, into but two "ages," or "æons," and that in connection with the "age to come" (αἰὼν μέλλων) the forgiveness of sin is excluded. This point was involved in another already given :

but in order to give the greater force to it, we present it here in a separate and explicit statement.

That the fact is as stated the Scriptures abundantly testify (Matt. xii, 32 ; xiii, 22 ; Mark iv, 19 ; x, 30; Luke xx, 35 ; Gal. i, 4 ; Eph. i, 21 ; ii, 7 ; 1 Tim. vi, 17 ; Tit. 2, 12). If the reader will examine these passages, he will find several phrases, ὁ αἰὼν οὗτος, ὁ αἰών, ὁ νῦν αἰών, ὁ ἐνεστὼς αἰών, used to signify the present life, and several others, αἰὼν μέλλων, ὁ αἰὼν ἐκεῖνος, ὁ αἰὼν ὁ ἐρχόμενος, οἱ αἰῶνες οἱ ἐπερχόμενοι, to signify the life to come ; and that the one set of phrases refers to the time before the advent (parousia) and the other to the time subsequent to that event.*

---

*Dr. W. E. Manly, to whom reference has been made, in his article in the *Arena* for April, 1890, seeks to prove that αἰὼν μέλλων in the New Testament, and the kindred phrases, refer to the Christian age about to be inaugurated in contradistinction to the Jewish age in which Christ and the apostles labored before the overthrow of the Jewish nation (A. D. 70). It is sufficient to say in response to this writer, and to all who teach the same doctrine from whatever stand-point, (1) That on this supposition one passage of Scripture, at least, is rendered both false and absurd. "And Jesus said unto them, The sons of this world (αἰῶνος τούτου) marry, and are given in marriage: but they that are accounted worthy to attain to that world (αἰῶνος ἐκείνου) and the resurrection from the dead, neither marry, nor are given in marriage : for neither can they die any more : for they are equal unto the angels ; and are sons of God.

15. Lastly, the fact that future restoration is not revealed in the Bible, and particularly in view of the facts already given, is probable proof of the endlessness of future punishment. This we think important. Some of the chief writers on the subject of restoration freely admit that the dogma is not revealed. Thus Farrar, however much he may contradict himself elsewhere, distinctly disavows being a Universalist: " But however deep may be our desire that this [universal restoration] should be the will of God; however beautifully it may seem to accord both with his mercy and his justice, that sin, after bringing its own punishment, should be turned to holiness, and so forgiven; however much we may cling to the hope that some such meaning may underlie the broad and boundless promises of a future restitution,—I dare not lay down any dogma of Universalism ; partly because it is not

---

being sons of the resurrection " (Luke xx, 34-36). (2) That " this age," in the language of Christ, did not refer to the Jewish age, but to the Christian dispensation already begun. This is shown by the use of the phrase in connection with several of the parables. For example, in reference to the " good seed" and the " tares " it is said, " Let both grow together until the harvest," and " the harvest is the end of the world " (συντέλεια αἰῶνος). Now this parable was spoken of "the kingdom of heaven," which corresponds with the Christian age (Matt. xiii, 24, 30, 39. See also same chap., ver. 22.)

clearly revealed to us, and partly because it is impossible for us to estimate the hardening effect of obstinate persistence in evil, and the power of the human will to resist the law and reject the love of God" (Preface to *Eternal Hope*, p. xvi, *et passim*, and in his later book, *Mercy and Judgment*). It is for him an "eternal hope," whatever that expression may mean. Whiton as distinctly disclaims any clear revelation as to restoration. He says: "The conclusion reached by this essay is, in general, that of nescience, namely, that the Bible, while teaching future punishment in terms sufficiently explicit and severe for the purposes of moral government, does not positively declare the duration of that punishment. An unbiased criticism by the best light that modern scholarship affords does not accept the sense which tradition has attached to some of the words of Scripture upon this subject. The Bible, however, reveals no restoration of 'the lost.' It casts no ray of hope upon the future of him who has wasted the present life" (*Is Eternal Punishment Endless?* p. xii of the Introduction). So, also, Martensen: "We only maintain that this solution [of what he calls an 'antinomy' in the Scriptures, according to which some passages seem to teach endless punishment and others restoration] is nowhere expressly given; and we ask whether we may not recognize divine wisdom in the fact that a final solution is not given us, while we are still in the stream of time and in the course of development?" (*Christian Dogmatics*, p. 476.) Likewise Dorner: "Accordingly, this hypothesis also [annihilationism] cannot lay claim to unreserved acknowledgment and dogmatic authority, and we must be content with saying that the ultimate fate of individuals remains veiled in mystery, as well as whether all will attain the blessed goal or not" (*System of Christian Doctrine*, vol. iv, p. 427).

Now we maintain that this silence, in view of the fact that the language of Scripture *seems*, to say the least, to teach the endlessness of punishment, is probable proof of that doctrine. We maintain this for the following reasons:

1. In view of the great amount and force of the evidence apparently for the doctrine in the Scriptures, if it is not true we are practically deceived. Martensen, in the quotation above, intimates that God needed to let us remain in doubt for our good. It amounts to saying that God needed to so speak to us in his word as to deceive us for our good, and is practically saying,

"God does evil that good may come of it"— Jesuit ethics hardly compatible with the divine character!

We readily grant that God can, consistently with his character, and does, reserve many things among the secrets of his counsel and ways; but this is very different from so revealing a doctrine as to cause it to deceive.* Shall the truth of God abound through *his* lie? "God forbid." The thought is dishonoring to God, and there is no alternative but to accept the doctrine as it appears, and has always appeared, to those who were willing to receive the manifest, and not some forced, interpretation of the divine Word.

2. May it not be said that if it were not so Christ would have told us, as he said concerning another matter, on the eve of his departure? (John xiv, 1.) This seems inevitable unless we are ready to accept the conclusion above drawn.

3. Uncertainty is practical certainty of restoration. This is so true that even those writers

---

* This is manifest, not only from what the above writers say, but also from the almost universal belief of Christendom in all the ages. Surely, if for eighteen centuries the Christian world has been persuaded of this doctrine, and the doctrine is not true, their deception is not surprising, and especially when the best that negative scholarship can do to-day is to claim a position of nescience or agnosticism.

who claim to be agnostics on the subject cherish such a large hope as to allay all alarm; and the hope they express is in many quarters proving an effective anæsthetic to many willing souls. The uncertainty of such writers is only *verbal;* the whole tenor and drift of their arguments is toward certainty of restoration. While Farrar disclaims Universalism, he nevertheless teaches it. Dr. Pusey points out this inconsistency in Farrar. He says: "It is difficult for another to understand the difference between a 'dogma* of Universalism' which the author 'dares not lay down,' and 'a hope' which is also 'a doctrine;' 'a truth,' '*truths*, which have been displaced by groundless *opinions*, and which are *necessary* for the purity, almost for the very existence, of that faith which is the one sole hope of the suffering world;' 'a doctrine which alone can stem the spread of infidelity;' essential to thinking 'noble thoughts of God'" (*What is of Faith as to Everlasting Punishment?* p. 26).

---

* A favorite device with many in the Church who teach what is contrary to the Scriptures is to shield themselves by claiming not to teach "dogma," but to hold "opinion." Witness the Andover heresy. It may be a legitimate thing to hold speculative opinions about non-essentials not revealed; but not so concerning such facts as probation and punishment, so essential and clearly revealed.

Thus, too, Whiton, whose positive assumptions are so modest as almost to disarm opposition, says: "But if any reader be inclined to complain, after reading this essay, that it has added nothing to things previously known, the writer would remind him that it is often as serviceable to the cause of truth to *define* the limits of our knowledge as to *extend* them. To be assured what one is *not* required to believe is often helpful to a doubt-encompassed soul, and vital to its victory in the conflict between faith and unbelief. Ignorant must he be of the phases of religious experience who does not know that in this way many a struggling swimmer may be lightened of a weight that threatens to engulf him in the depths of infidelity" (*Is "Eternal" Punishment Endless?* p. xiii). Surely, if one is *not* required to believe the doctrine, and the doubt so necessary that "many a struggling swimmer may be lightened of a weight that threatens to engulf him in the depths of infidelity" may be entertained, the result is, practically, restorationism, so far as faith is concerned. Clearly, the Bible cannot leave us in the doubt that begets such inconsistency. The fact is, there is no middle position, except in assertion, between belief of the doctrine and unbelief. The conclusion is inevitable; the doctrine is a terrible reality; and instead of in fact holding out a delusive hope under the modest assumption of "nescience," the doctrine should be proclaimed (if ever so unpleasant, as it must be to all who sincerely proclaim it), and all should take the warning it involves.

We have now completed a survey of all the leading evidence that we think can fairly be urged as furnishing ground for the doctrine. We might have given quotations from the Old Testament; but have not done so for the reason that we think Old Testament evidence is subsidiary and of secondary importance, and we have been giving that which is primary and conclusive. We must read the Old Testament teaching in the light of the New. There are a few other points, however, that may be briefly mentioned as furnishing corroboration to the proof already adduced.

1. The first point is that the Jews in Christ's day believed in the endlessness of the punishment of the wicked, so that speaking to his disciples as Christ did they could not get any other impression from the unqualified language that he used. We do not mean to affirm that this was the only doctrine held by the Jews of Christ's time, but that it *was* held. Dr. Pusey says:

" Belief in the eternity of future punishment is contained in the Book of Judith, in the fourth Book of Maccabees, in the so-called Psalms of Solomon: the second death is mentioned in the Targums of Onkelos and Jonathan : Josephus attests the belief of the Pharisees and the Essenes in the eternity of punishment" (*What is of Faith*, etc., p. 50). These books to which Dr. Pusey refers were written before or soon after the time of our Lord. So, also, Edersheim, who is a master in this field of research, concerning the teaching immediately before the time of Christ of the schools of Shammai and Hillel, says: " The former arranged all mankind into three classes: the perfectly righteous, who are 'immediately written and sealed to eternal life ; ' the perfectly wicked, who are ' immediately written and sealed to Gehenna ; ' and an intermediate class, who ' go down to Gehinnom, and moan, and come up again,' according to Zech. xiii, 9, and which seemed also indicated in certain words in the song of Hannah (1 Sam. ii, 6). The careful reader will notice that this statement implies belief in eternal punishment on the part of the school of Shammai. For (1) the perfectly wicked are spoken of as ' written and sealed unto Gehenna ; ' (2) the school of Shammai expressly quotes, in support of what it teaches about these wicked, Dan. xii, 2, a passage which undoubtedly refers to the final judgment after the resurrection; (3) the perfectly wicked, so punished, are expressly distinguished from the third, or intermediate class, who merely 'go down to Gehinnom' but are not 'written and sealed,' and 'come up again'" (*Life and Times of Jesus the Messiah*, Appendix to vol. ii, p. 792). Now, in view of this fact, how is it possible to understand Christ's language on the subject (Matt. xxv, 46; Mark ix, 43-48, *et al.*) with the hope of final restoration of all men to life and happiness? His listeners could not mistake his meaning.*

2. The fact of endless punishment is confirmed by the fact of the atonement. We say *confirmed*, not proved; for conceivably Christ, in mercy, might have suffered and died to deliver from the limited future punishment that is said, even by Restorationists,† to await the im-

---

* If the reader desires further to examine the question pro and contra concerning the belief of the Jews on this subject, let him consult the recent works upon it, especially those of Pusey and Farrar (*ut supra*), and also the work of Dr. Love, *Future Probation Examined*, chap. vii. Also, Schürer's *The Jewish People in the Time of Jesus Christ*, vol. ii, pp. 181-183.

† Many of these make the punishment of the wicked to last for "ages upon ages." We here take no account of the logical and theological inconsistency that attributes the salvation of men to Christ *after* the penalty.

penitent in the other world. But the endlessness of future punishment more easily and fully explains the infinite sacrifice of Christ.

3. So, also, the apparent need of the doctrine confirms the other evidence of its reality. The familiar saying that the "fear of hell peoples heaven" has some force, if not as much as is sometimes claimed for it.

Are there not already signs of religious decay as a result of the decline of faith in this doctrine? Besides, the fact is that a decline of evangelical faith and religion has accompanied, and is to-day accompanying, the dissemination of this error. Universalism is of close kin to Unitarianism (*History of Rationalism*, by Bishop John F. Hurst, pp. 560, 561). On the other hand, the most aggressive Christian work has been, and is to-day being, done by the Churches that accept the doctrine, as, for example, witness our own Church.

4. The last confirmatory argument that we give is the belief of the Church. Our claim for this is of the slightest character. Of itself it would amount to nothing; but in connection with the other facts given it is of some weight. We are not ready to say the great mass of Christian believers, both before and since the Ref-

ormation, have been deceived on this subject, except in the light of the clearest proof.

In conclusion, let it be said that the arguments presented corroborate and strengthen each other, and that the entire force of the proof of this doctrine is not in the single points presented, however strong these may be, but in the combined strength of each and all together. When thus considered we do not see how, from exegetical considerations, the doctrine can be honestly denied.

"Because with lies ye have made the heart of the righteous sad, whom I have not made sad; and strengthened the hands of the wicked, that he should not return from his wicked way, by promising him life."—Ezek. xiii, 22.

"Which say to the seers, See not; and to the prophets, Prophesy not unto us right things, speak unto us smooth things, prophesy deceits."—Isa. xxx, 10.

CHAPTER II.

Objections and Arguments of Restorationists.

THE objections to the doctrine of future endless retribution are said to be both rational and scriptural. We propose in the present place to notice the most important of these in this order, namely, (I) those that are urged from reason and (II) those that are accounted scriptural.

I. OBJECTIONS FROM REASON.

1. First, under this category, is to be named the objection from justice. The objection in brief is as follows: God cannot be unjust, and he, therefore, cannot punish the wicked forever. It is seldom or never urged in this direct manner; but, disrobed of all its rhetorical dress and made to stand clearly before the mind as it is, it is thus properly expressed. It has two wholly different propositions (with an enormous assumption for a minor premise) that need to be kept thoroughly apart in our thought or treatment of the subject. The first proposition—that God cannot be unjust—no one will dispute. We know this because

of his character as revealed in his Word: "Righteousness and judgment are the foundation of thy throne" (Psa. lxxxix, 14). "Righteous and true are thy ways, thou King of the ages" (Rev. xv, 3). Nor is his justice based upon his might, but upon his character. God has a right to do as he pleases; but, happily for us, he pleases to do the right. "God is love." Upon his love is built his justice. Neither is his justice some abstract, metaphysical quality wholly unlike the same sentiment in ourselves.* We fully accept the fact that God's sentiment of both justice and love is the same in kind as ours. The difference is in degree only. God is perfect and we imperfect. The same is true of all the corresponding attributes of each.

The second proposition would be true only on the ground of the assumed truthfulness of the suppressed minor premise, in the argument, namely, that it would be unjust in God to punish sin in this life with endless suffering. But, clearly,

---

* Canon Row devotes much of his argument from reason against future endless punishment to the refutation of this false conception of the sentiment of justice in God, and to the refutation of the same view of the love of God. It is safe to say that this is the position of but few Christian writers, and that the Christian Church has always accepted, with Dr. Row, the sameness in kind of the divine attributes with those of all moral intelligences. (See Row's *Future Retribution*, pp. 20-27.)

this is the thing to be proved. Nor has any one done so, and for the manifest reason that it is beyond the range of proof. We are not familiar enough with the facts involved to be able rationally to decide the matter; and, in view of the manifest teaching of the Scriptures as to the endlessness of future punishment, it becomes us to "Stand in awe, and sin not." The question is not one of justice, but of *knowledge;* and, clearly, we are not in the position to know the guilt and necessary punishment of sin. Omniscience alone is equal to such knowledge, and the knowledge can become ours not by *insight*, but alone by *revelation*. What the revelation is we have seen in the foregoing chapter.

We venture a few remarks that may throw some light upon this subject:

(1) The guilt and necessary punishment of sin are to be viewed in the light of man's greatness and responsibility as revealed in the Bible. If man is simply a highly developed animal, with no more or little more freedom than the intelligent brute, then the matter of eternal guilt and punishment is clearly untenable; but if as to his spirit man has the "image of God," as is taught in the Scriptures, and is a free moral agent in any proper sense of the phrase, then, clearly,

eternal guilt and eternal punishment, in view of the necessity of the latter, are not contradictory or absurd. Man's greatness has something to do with his eternal guilt in deliberate sin.

It is to be observed that all Restorationists more or less excuse man's guilt.

(2) Further light is thrown upon this subject in view of the fact that sin is committed against God. We are not prepared to affirm, with Dr. Shedd, that sin against an infinite being *must* have infinite guilt. We have no knowledge of the Infinite and of sin to justify us in such an assumption. But we are prepared to say simply that sinning against God adds culpability to our sin. For the rest we can adopt the words of the eminent author just referred to: "To torture a dumb beast is a crime; to torture a man is a greater crime. To steal from one's own mother is more heinous than to steal from a fellow-citizen. The person who transgresses is the same in each instance; but the different worth and dignity of the objects upon whom his action terminates makes the difference in the gravity of the two offenses. David's adultery was a finite evil in reference to Uriah, but an infinite evil [we prefer to say, 'much greater evil,' not because we know that it was not infinite, but because we do *not*

know, from this stand-point, that it was] in reference to God. 'Against thee only have I sinned,' was the feeling of the sinner in this case. Had the patriarch Joseph yielded, he would have sinned against Pharaoh. But the greatness of the sin as related to the fellow-creature is lost in its enormity as related to the Creator, and his only question is: 'How can I do this great wickedness and sin against God?'" (*Dogmatic Theology*, vol. ii, p. 740.)

(3) Another fact that throws light upon the subject is that guilt must last forever. If a man commits a crime he may pay the penalty that human law has attached to it, and conceivably that that divine law has attached to it,* and yet the fact and guilt of sin remain. Even a sinner forgiven is a forgiven *sinner;* the fact and guilt of his sin can never be canceled. In all eternity we believe the saved will be conscious that they are sinners saved from uncanceled guilt. We speak of sin and guilt as canceled or destroyed, and in popular language it expresses a glorious redemptive truth—the truth of forgiveness—but in fact and from a metaphysical stand-point both are never-ending.

---

* This is said with the momentary conjecture that the penalty is limited in duration.

2. The objection from the divine love. We stop simply for a moment to consider the objection urged from this stand-point. It is said that God cannot suffer a soul to perish forever; that his infinite love will cause him to follow the last lost sheep into the wilderness until he find it.

To this we reply that it is in God not a matter of disposition, but a matter of ability. We have no hesitancy in saying that if God could he would save the last lost soul in the universe, and that he would spare no cost to do so. But we have all reason for believing that all his divine resources for the salvation of men are exhausted in the infinite sacrifice of the cross; that when God gave his Son for the world's redemption he exhausted the infinite treasury of grace and power, and that no other terms of salvation could be proposed than those given in the Scriptures.

The necessity of future punishment we reserve for a separate treatment (chap. viii).

It may be further said in response to this objection that it may be urged with equal plausibility, and in fact is so urged by the infidel, against the divine providential ordering and governing of this world. Except in the face of facts we would be equally inclined to object to many things in this world as incompatible with the character of a benevolent Creator. But facts are stubborn things, and we have to reconcile them as best we can. So, also, is this revealed fact of endless retribution. Butler long ago pointed out this analogy, and it is needless to dwell upon it longer.

3. The objection from the divine omniscience. It is sometimes urged that the foreknowledge of God, in view of his love, is incompatible with the fact of endless punishment; that God, foreknowing that some would be lost forever, would have refrained from creating the human race. Some, to evade this difficulty, as well as the difficulty of evil in general in the universe, deny to God the foreknowledge of contingent events. But without denying this scriptural fact we may advance in mitigation of the difficulty the following facts: (1) The creation of man was a benevolent act. (2) While man is not responsible for the inclination to sin with which he is born, he, nevertheless, having sufficient grace given him whereby to overcome this and all actual sin if he choose, is responsible for actual sin. Man is a free being. (3) God, in creating the race of men, intended *all* to be saved (2 Pet. iii, 9). (4) None will be lost but those who *will not* be saved (John v, 40). Damnation is a thing of deliberate choice.

(5) The race, as such, will in all probability be saved. (This point will be dwelt upon in a subsequent chapter, v.)

With these qualifications the objections from this stand-point vanish. It is by forgetting or ignoring them, especially man's freedom, that the objections find place.

4. The objection from teleology. The objection from this stand-point asks, with Martensen, the almost stunning question : " Must this world's development, then, end in a dualism?" Will evil continue forever in a benevolent universe along with the good?

It is one of the most serious difficulties with which the doctrine of future retribution has to contend; but, however difficult and startling the thought may be, it can weigh nothing against a clearly revealed fact of the divine Word. Besides, as Dorner, who certainly is not biased toward the orthodox doctrine, says, " The objective reason why no categorical affirmation [concerning apokatastasis] can be made on dogmatic grounds lies in human *freedom*. It does not admit the assertion of a universal process leading *necessarily* to salvation, because such process is and remains conditioned by non-rejection and free acceptance" (*System of Christian Doctrine*, vol. iv, p. 424);

only we would limit the influence of freedom to this life in deciding destiny. The further reason of this eternal dualism will be discussed in another place (chap. viii).

Other objections of this class, more or less involved in those already given, need not be considered.

II. OBJECTIONS FROM THE SCRIPTURES.

All the objections from this stand-point are urged chiefly with reference to the word αἰώνιος in Matt. xxv, 46, and such phrases as "eternal fire" (τὸ πῦρ τὸ αἰώνιον), "unquenchable fire" (τὸ πῦρ τὸ ἀσβεστον), "unto ages" (εἰς αἰῶνα), "unto the ages of ages" (εἰς τοὺς αἰῶνας τῶν αἰώνων), etc.

1. As to the word αἰώνιος in Matthew, it is asserted by some that it cannot mean eternal; by others, simply that it does not mean eternal. Both assertions are made, so far as we have been able to judge, principally on the ground that in *some* cases, and *etymologically*, it does not mean eternal. We know no writer who pretends to assert in either case the contrary. On the other hand, they all acknowledge that αἰών—the substantive form of which αἰώνιος is a derivative adjective—etymologically means an "age," and

that αἰώνιος itself is often used both in the Greek writers, in the Septuagint (where it is used in the translation of the Hebrew עוֹלָם, a word that has in the Old Testament an almost parallel signification with the word αἰών in its uses in the New Testament; due, no doubt, to the fact that the New Testament writers used the Septuagint version of the older Scriptures), and in the New Testament in the sense of limited duration. But the question to be considered is whether it *ever* means "eternal."

Those who assert that the word never means eternal do so in the face of many indubitable facts to the contrary. From the Scriptures we insist that it does so mean in reference to God and the future life of the righteous. (Examine Rom. xvi, 26; 2 Cor. iv, 17; v, 1; Heb. v, 9; ix, 15.) Lexicographers also tell us that the word has in some instances the same meaning in the Greek classics. (See Thayer, *Greek-English Lexicon of the New Testament, in loco.**)

The particular question, then, for us to con-

---

* It will not detract from the argument to remind the reader that the word "eternal" is not only a translation of the Greek αἰώνιος, but that it is identical with it. "The Greek αἰών (æon) is one and the same with the Latin *ævum*, and from this we get *ævitas* and *æviternus*, with their shortened forms, *ætas* and *æternus.*"

sider is, Does the word mean eternal in this place? That it does may be inferred not only from the fact that there is no reason for the assertion to the contrary, but also from the correlated facts adduced in the Scripture proofs of the doctrine of punishment (chap. 1).

2. As to the phrases "unto ages," "unto the ages of ages," etc., it is sometimes said that they cannot signify "eternal," for no amount of multiplication of "ages" can make an eternity.

Our response to this is that these plural forms and phrases are rhetorical expressions intended to emphasize and deepen the impression of eternity, like our own "for ever and ever." And that they signify absolute endlessness it is surprising that any one can deny. That they do so signify is manifest from the following Scriptures: "If any man eat of this bread, he shall live forever" (εἰς τὸν αἰῶνα) (John vi, 51). "He that eateth this bread shall live forever" (John vi, 58). "Thy throne, O God, is for ever and ever" (εἰς τὸν αἰῶνα τοῦ αἰῶνος) (Heb. i, 8). "And they shall reign for ever and ever" (εἰς τοὺς αἰῶνας τῶν αἰώνων) (Rev. xxii, 5).

3. Concerning the phrase "eternal fire," it is objected: Even if the word αἰώνιος here does mean "eternal," still the phrase signifies nothing

as to the eternity of punishment, for it is the "fire" that is eternal and not the punishment, the instrument of punishment and not the punishment itself. The same is said with reference to the phrases " unquenchable fire," " the fire is not quenched," etc.

It is sufficient to reply to this that such is not the impression that one naturally gets from reading this terrible language. The words have to be *explained* to mean this. And again, unless the " fire " of future punishment in the New Testament represents some external instrument of torture (a thing that few Universalists will be willing to admit), it cannot last forever. Otherwise, it must in the nature of things cease to be when the punishment ceases. Besides, if it be even thought that the instrument *is* external, it is inconceivable that it shall continue forever, its function and use having come to an end.

" Eternal" and " unquenchable" fire can mean nothing less, therefore, than eternal punishment.

4. It is asserted further by some that the word αἰώνιος in the New Testament connotates a *qualitative* and not a *quantitative* meaning; that " eternal life " signifies the kind of life those in Christ enjoy, and has no reference to its duration ; and that " eternal punishment " signifies the kind

of punishment the wicked must endure, and has no reference to its duration. For the Christian not versed in Greek and not used to scientific study it may be looked upon simply as "figurative" (Whiton, *Is " Eternal" Punishment Endless?* p. xii).

We content ourselves in response with a single remark, namely, that not only does the quantitative sense of the word suit the connection in all cases in which it is used in the New Testament (*Biblical Eschatology*, A. Hovey, p. 163); and not only is the word "life" used by John to signify the quality of our existence in Christ without the word "eternal" (John iii, 36; v, 24; vi, 33, etc.); but that in none of the instances of its use is the impression naturally made that the word has the qualitative signification. The word that expresses quality of existence in Christ in the phrase "eternal life" is the word "life," and the word "eternal" simply governs the life as to its duration. When St. John speaks of "eternal life" as a present possession, and St. Paul speaks of it as a hope (Rom. ii, 7; Tit. i, 2; iii, 7), the thought is in every case "the life which is eternal," the first word signifying the quality and the second the quantity or duration of existence.

Another form of this same objection is that which asserts that the word αἰώνιος signifies simply "pertaining to eternity." This also, however, will not bear the test of the laws of lexicography.

Still another form of the objection is that which asserts that the word has an "absolute" signification; that in its use in the Scriptures it denotes that which is *above* time. The objection in this form is associated with the notion that time and eternity are exclusive ideas, and that with regard to God and eternal things it is not proper to postulate succession or duration of existence. On this ground it is asserted that when the word αἰώνιος is used with reference to the life after death it signifies nothing as to duration, and hence that it signifies nothing as to the extent of future punishment.

In response to this it will be sufficient to quote the following words of Plumptre, a well-known scholar of the first rank, and one whose testimony will not be thought to favor through traditional prejudice the common view. As to the word αἰώνιος, after referring to many instances of its use in the New Testament, he says: "It might seem as if this were a sufficient induction to establish the conclusion that the word served to express the fullest thought that man could grasp of absolute limitless duration " (*The Spirits in Prison*, p. 361). As to the thought of time being eliminated from the thought of eternity in the Scriptures, he says: "I find it impossible to conceive of life, either human or divine, apart from the idea of duration," and then shows from such passages as Rev. i, 8; Psa. cxxxv, 13; cxxxvi, 1-26, that, separate from the word αἰώνιος, the idea of duration is expressly given in connection with the idea of the divine Being (*ibid.*, p. 368. The whole connection will repay examination).

III. Arguments of Universalists.

We next turn to the most important arguments of the Universalist, by which he seeks to establish his pleasing claim. Many arguments from this source are too artificial to deserve serious notice. Those which we propose to examine are of two kinds: (I) Those urged from specific passages of Scripture, and (II) those that claim to be legitimate deductions from certain general principles.

A preliminary word as to method. Few writers of this class have any regard for sound laws of exegesis. In the matter of specific texts, in nearly all cases the context is wholly ignored. Few, however, are so outspoken in their disregard for particular passages of Scripture as is Dr. Cox in the following quotation :

"For myself I am glad that this necessary, yet less welcome and less conclusive, part of our task is over, and that we may pass on and up from these minute critical investigations to breathe a larger air and to move freely along a higher path. For not only does it cramp and deaden the spirit that is in man to tarry long in the low valley of mere criticism, where the atmosphere is commonly charged with the elements of polemical strife; but it is also impossible for him, until he climb up out of it, to gain any broad, decisive, and inspiring view of the truth for which he contends. For no conclusion can be safely based on the study of scattered and isolated texts;" by which he means particular passages of Scripture, such as he has already examined (*Salvator Mundi*, p. 148).

Before passing to the more particular consideration of our present topic, we beg leave to remind the Universalist who claims so much for principles, and who has so little regard for specific texts, that all his so-called principles are but inductions from particular statements of the divine Word. What, for example, is the principle of divine love but an induction from such passages of Scripture as " For God so loved the world, that he gave his only begotten Son, that whosoever believeth on him should not perish, but have eternal life," and "God is love?" Or, again, what is the principle of the divine " unchangeableness " but an induction from such passages as these : " For I the Lord change not " (Mal. iii, 6), " Every good gift and every perfect boon is from above, coming down from the Father of lights, with whom can be no variation, neither shadow that is cast by turning" (Jas. i, 17)? We would remind the Universalist still further that these so-called principles of his are not, properly speaking, principles at all, but revealed facts; or, if he insists on saying they are revealed principles, we reply that endless suffering is as much a revealed principle, on this assumption, as is the divine love or unchangeableness. We prefer to say, however, that they are revealed facts, all of them ; and whether we stand on the summit or not from which we can see their harmony and reconciliation, as revealed they are to be accepted in our thinking and life, and should govern our teaching and conduct.

Furthermore, we can have no controversy upon the subject with those whose method is to subordinate the teaching of Scripture to the so-called dictates of reason and the moral sense. We are not rationalists, and are unwilling to apply in practice a principle which we ignore in profession. Our only contention, then, will be with those who claim to get their specific teaching and principles of reasoning from the divine Word.

I. Arguments from so-called principles, or deductions from undisputed Scripture facts.

1. First among these we place that which is urged on the ground of the divine unchangeableness. This argument has various forms and illustrations, but in substance asserts that since God is unchangeable, and has dealt with men in the past, and deals with them in the present, on certain principles of mercy and patience, he will always so deal with them, and hence that the door of grace will never be closed upon their return to life and happiness.

The insuperable difficulty with the argument, however, is that it proves too much; for if the final restoration of all men is a legitimate inference on the ground of the divine unchangeableness from the principle and fact of past and present dealings of mercy, then equally may eternal wrath be deduced, on the same ground, from the fact that in this life in certain instances the door of repentance has been closed upon the persistently wicked. Witness, for example, the antediluvians who perished in the flood, and Esau (Heb. xii, 17), besides the many cases in which the door of return has been closed, and is being closed to-day, upon those who have forfeited or wasted their powers and opportunities, as seen outside of the Scriptures. The fact is, the divine unchangeableness proves no more than what is revealed concerning it, and this is consistent with the equally revealed fact of punishment. Moreover, the divine unchangeableness, in view of the Scriptures which affirm that sin persisted in conducts to an irretrievable ruin, is to be urged with all its force on the side of the teaching of the orthodox Church. Because God who changes not has declared, " The soul that sinneth, it shall die," therefore we accept the plain and terrible teaching of the divine Word, and urge men to immediate repentance. Any other use of this fact, in view of all that is revealed, is wresting the Scriptures to one's own destruction (2 Pet. iii, 16).

2. The divine love. We have sufficiently considered this in another place, and stop here to add a word only. There can be no contention between the Universalist and the orthodox believer at this point.* The love of God is as

---
* We mean, of course, the Trinitarian Universalist.

much a cherished fact to the one as to the other. We both measure the love of God in the light of the cross. The difference between us is in our inferential assertion from this fact. The Universalist says, " God is love; therefore he will ultimately save all men." We say, " God is love, and desires to save all men, but cannot save those who in life will not be saved." The reason of future endless retribution, as before intimated, will be considered later on.

3. Sufficient has also been said concerning the divine justice.

4. Another fact which is virtually (Martensen), and sometimes actually (Jukes), urged as an argument in favor of final universal restoration is what is called by some an " antinomy " in the Scriptures, and by others an " apparent contradiction." Sometimes this so-called antinomy, or apparent contradiction, is attempted to be explained, and in the interest of restoration; again, it is left unexplained with a secret hope that beneath the mystery lies a deep purpose of benevolence that will finally compass the salvation of all men. The facts on which this doctrine is built may best be stated in the language of its advocates.

"This antinomy meets us if we turn to the

Holy Scriptures, and no definite solution is given of it there. There are texts which, if they be taken in their full and literal import, most distinctly refer to eternal damnation. When the Lord speaks of 'everlasting fire, prepared for the devil and his angels;' when he speaks of 'the worm that dieth not, and the fire which shall not be quenched;' when he mentions sins against the Holy Ghost, which 'shall never be forgiven, neither in this world, nor in that which is to come' (Mark ix, 43; Matt. xii, 32); when the apostle John declares that there is a sin unto death, for which a man must not pray (1 John v, 16),—these texts, if they be taken without reservation or refinement, clearly express the idea of a condemnation in which there is no cessation, to which there is no end. But, on the other hand, there are contrasted expressions of Scripture which have an equal claim to be taken in their full sense. When the apostle Paul says that 'the *last* enemy that shall be destroyed is death' (therefore the other, the second death; because otherwise there would still remain an unconquerable enemy); when he speaks of the time 'when God shall be all in all' (1 Cor. xv, 26-28), without referring to any contrast whatever between blessed and condemned; when he states, without any reservations, that 'all things shall be gathered together in Christ' (Eph. i, 10) as the Head, that 'as in Adam *all* die, even so in Christ shall *all* be made alive' (1 Cor. xv, 22),—if we take these texts without limiting their full and obvious import, we shall not be far from the idea of a universal restoration; for the apostle says expressly ALL, not some. (Compare Matt. xix, 26.) This apparent contradiction in the language of Scripture shows that Scripture itself does not afford us a final dogmatic solution of the question. He who seeks to establish the doctrine of (ἀποκατάστασις) universal restoration must invalidate those texts which make mention of eternal damnation, must limit and pare them down according to this idea; and he who would establish eternal damnation as a dogma by means of Scripture is obliged to limit and pare down those texts which speak for the ἀποκατάστασις, according to this idea: for example, when the apostle says, 'As in Adam all die, even so in Christ shall all be made alive,' he must explain the second 'all' as meaning 'some,' and he must take the first 'all' in a particular and equally restricted sense. We readily grant that the Word of God cannot contradict itself, and that the antinomy here presented must really be solved in the depth of God's Word. We only maintain that this solution is nowhere expressly given; and we ask whether we may not recognize divine wisdom in the fact that a final solution is not given us, while we are still in the stream of time and in the course of development?" (Martensen, *Christian Dogmatics*, pp. 475, 476.)

Again: "What, then, does Scripture say on this subject? Its testimony appears at first sight contradictory. Not only is there on the one hand law, condemning all, while on the other hand there is the Gospel, with good news for every one; but, further, there are direct statements as to the results of these, which at first sight are apparently irreconcilable. First our Lord calls his flock 'a little flock,' and states distinctly that 'many are called, but few are chosen;' that 'strait is the ,gate, and narrow is the way, which leadeth unto life, and few there be that find it;' that 'many shall seek to enter in, and shall not be able;' that while 'he that believeth on the Son hath everlasting life, he that believeth not the Son shall not see life, but the wrath of God abideth on him;' that 'the wicked shall go away into everlasting punishment,' 'prepared for the devil and his angels;'

'the resurrection of damnation;' 'the damnation of hell,' 'where their worm dieth not, and the fire is not quenched;' that though 'every word against the Son of man may be forgiven, the sin against the Holy Ghost shall not be forgiven, neither in this world, nor in that which is to come;' and that of one at least it is true, that 'good had it been for that man if he had not been born.'

* * * * *

"Words could not well be stronger. The difficulty is that all this is but one side of Scripture, which in other places seems to teach a very different doctrine. For instance, there are first the words of God himself, repeated again and again by those same apostles whom I have just quoted, that 'in Abraham's seed all the kindreds of the earth shall be blessed'—words which St. Peter expounds to mean that there shall be 'a restitution of all things,' adding that 'God hath spoken of this by the mouth of all his holy prophets since the world began.' St. Paul further declares this wondrous 'mystery of God's will, that he hath purposed in himself, according to his good pleasure, to rehead and reconcile unto himself, in and by Christ, all things, whether they be things in heaven'—that is, the spirit-world, where the conflict with Satan yet is—

'or things on earth'—that is, this outward world, where death now reigns, and where even God's elect are by nature children of wrath, even as other men. Further, St. Paul asserts that 'all creation, which now groans, shall be delivered from the bondage of corruption, into the glorious liberty of the children of God.' In another place he declares that 'God was in Christ reconciling the world unto himself,' and that Christ 'took our flesh and blood, through death to destroy him that had the power of death, that is, the devil;' that 'if by the offense of one many be dead, much more the grace of God and the gift by grace, which is by one man, Jesus Christ, hath abounded unto many;' that 'therefore as by the offense of one, or by one offense, judgment came on all to condemnation, even so by the righteousness of one, or by one righteousness, the free gift should come on all unto justification of life,' while 'they which receive abundance of grace, and of the gift of righteousness, shall reign in life by one, Jesus Christ;' that 'as sin hath reigned unto death, so grace might reign unto eternal life,' yea, that 'where sin abounded, grace did yet much more abound. . . .'

" . . . What can this contradiction mean? Is there any key, and if so, what is it, to this mystery?" (Jukes, *Restitution of All Things*, pp. 19–26.)

The key that this writer finds is the doctrine of universal restoration.

As to the alleged antinomy we can offer nothing better than the following from a writer already quoted:

"There is a sophism in the very word. In a pure question of fact the term 'antinomy' is not applicable. It can properly apply only to the relation existing between two laws or principles (principles either of procedure or of thought) which are each conceived as valid and imperative, but which issue in contradictory propositions. Now, of course, it is allowable to argue the purely *a priori* question: Do our conceptions of God, or of the moral nature of man, necessitate a belief that the punishment of human sin will be endless? Such an argument may issue in a so-called 'antinomy of faith.' But the question in hand is one of fact. The mind may remain at rest in an antinomy; it does not, at least, annul organic thought. It is compatible with reason and science. The instance given above is familiar; divine foreknowledge on the one hand, human responsibility on the other. It is otherwise with a question of fact—the existence and non-existence at the same time of a given thing, the taking place and the not taking place of a given event. The present question is one of the latter kind—one on which the Scriptures do not *reason* with men, but *announce* to men " (William A. Stevens, in the *Bibliotheca Sacra*, January, 1889, p. 139).

But allowing the word "antinomy" to stand, if thereby is intended an "apparent contradiction," as others affirm, we are prepared to assert that there is no such "apparent contradiction" between the passages cited except to those who persistently ignore their plain and obvious intent as seen when read in their connections. Consideration will be given to these specific passages in another place (pp. 91-113).

5. Punishment remedial. It is asserted that in the Scriptures future punishment is set forth as corrective, remedial, and hence that it will cease when it has fulfilled its function in disciplining the lost for heaven. This is sometimes asserted as an inference from the fact of a divine benevolent chastisement in the present life (Heb. xii, 5-11). Again, the assertion is made on the ground of certain Scripture words and statements. We propose to consider the validity or invalidity of the claim.

So far as the teaching is an inference from such Scriptures as Heb. xii, 5-11, it is plainly in conflict with the logical requirement which demands the ground of the inference. We gladly recognize the revealed fact that our heavenly Father chastens his children for their profit in this life, but see nothing in this to invalidate the fact, equally revealed, of future punishment that, because eternal, cannot be corrective. Besides, the "chastisement" of the Bible is for "sons," and sinners are not sons in the evangelical use of the word. (Compare John viii, 44; Rom. viii, 14; Gal. iv, 5, 6.)

As to Scripture facts directly claimed in its favor, it is said that the word κόλασις in the phrase "eternal punishment" (κόλασιν αἰώνιον) in Matt. xxv, 46, signifies "pruning," or discipline, and that the wicked are accordingly assigned in the judgment to an "æonial pruning," not punishment. It is claimed that the true Greek word for "retributive" punishment is τιμωρία, not κόλασις.

It is freely acknowledged that the alleged distinction is made in the classic Greek writings. (See Thayer, *ut supra*.) But even in these writings "usage does not always recognize the distinction," especially in the later of them (*ibid.*).

Also, κόλασις is used in the Septuagint in some instances (for example, 2 Macc. iv, 38), and once at least in the verb form in the New Testament (Acts iv, 21), where the idea of discipline is excluded. The first of these passages concerns the punishment of Andronicus by Antiochus for the murder of the high-priest Onias, and is as follows: "And being kindled with anger, forthwith he took away Andronicus his pupil, and rent off his clothes, and leading him through the whole city unto that very place where he had committed impiety against Onias, there slew he the cursed murderer. Thus the Lord rewarded him his punishment [κόλασιν] as he had deserved." The passage in Acts is as follows: "And they, when they had further threatened them, let them go, finding nothing how they might punish [κολάσωνται] them, because of the people." Moreover, there is no instance of the use of the word in the Bible where the retributive sense is not perfectly natural, and in fact only so. (Compare 1 John iv, 18; 2 Pet. ii, 9.) The word that properly signifies discipline is παιδεία. Again, κόλασις is not alone used in the Scriptures of the punishment of the wicked. In Heb. x, 29, it is asked, "Of how much sorer punishment [τιμωρίας], think ye, shall he be judged worthy, who hath trodden under foot the Son of God, and hath counted the blood of the covenant, wherewith he was sanctified, an unholy thing, and hath done despite unto the Spirit of grace?"

Again, it is asserted that the remedial character of future punishment is taught in the use of the word "fire," which describes its nature, and especially in the phrase "salted with fire" in Mark ix, 49. It is said one of the functions of fire, and especially "salt," is to purify, or cleanse, and that these words intimate the purging quality of the punishment of the life to come, which purging will go on until all the moral filth of the universe is burned up. When sin is thus burned out of the souls of men, then they will be ready for the purity of heaven. It is intimated that the fires of Hinnom (γέεννα), the place which symbolized the future place of torment, were kindled and kept burning for sanitary purposes.

In response to this we may say, first, that no doubt fire has a sanitary function, and that the fire of hell has the same function for the moral world; but it is for the purgation of the moral *world*, and not of those cast into it. The fire of Hinnom kept the pestilence from the city of Jerusalem; it did not cleanse, but *destroyed* the things cast into it. Moreover, fire was used in some instances for purely punitive purposes (Lev. x, 2; Num. xvi, 35).

The phrase "salted with fire" is somewhat different, and yet it is with little consistency that writers of this school lay so much emphasis upon so "isolated" and figurative an expression. Besides, it is not admitted by all that the words refer to the future life at all; and if they do, it must be remembered that the sacrifice (to which allusion is made, see Lev. ii, 13) was not salted for its own sake, but as a symbol of cleansing for the people. For further consideration of this most difficult passage, the reader must be referred to the various commentaries and kindred works.

Another fact that is urged to prove that the future punishment of the wicked is remedial is that which is recorded in First Corinthians, fifth chapter and fifth verse, concerning the offender who was to be delivered unto Satan for the destruction of the flesh, that his spirit might be saved in the day of the Lord Jesus. (Compare 1 Tim. i, 20.) It is said that "this wretched Corinthian *was*, as we know, redeemed by his very condemnation, and delivered *from* the power of the devil by being delivered *into* the power of the devil" (2 Cor. ii, 5-11). The inference is made from this case that when the wicked are delivered unto Satan in the judgment it is with a like beneficent purpose.

In response, besides referring to tne unwarranted assumption which bases a doctrine of the future life upon God's dealings with men in this life, we may say: (1) The express object of the present deliverance unto Satan of this man was that the flesh might be destroyed and the spirit "saved *in the day of the Lord Jesus.*" Why this present concern except on the assumption that without the present destruction of the flesh the spirit would be *lost* in the day of the Lord Jesus? (2) Being delivered unto Satan could not mean the same as "cast into the lake of fire" "prepared for the devil and his angels." The act of the Corinthian Church was an ecclesiastical act of excommunication. This seems to have been the import of the phrase "deliver such a one unto Satan," so far as the Corinthian society had to do with the matter. Surely that Church had no other power. By this excommunication, and consequent surrendering of this wicked one unto Satan, whom he had already been serving, or, in other words, by the rebuke of the Church, and being left to the unrestrained working of the lust of the flesh, Paul hoped (and he did not hope in vain) that the fallen brother might be restored.

But we have a dogmatic controversy with this doctrine. If future punishment is remedial, what did Christ die to redeem us from ? Surely not from a *necessary* remedy ; and Universalists such as Mr. Cox say that future punishment is necessary as a remedy. But they say future punishment is also retributive. Then, are we saved from the retributive element of punishment, and left to endure it for the remedial effect? Shall we thus split the intent of future punishment? And if so, what effect of sin are we *practically* redeemed from ? What is the retributive element of future punishment as separate from the remedial in the punishment itself? We can conceive the twofold intent of punishment, but cannot conceive a redemption from an *intent* while the punishment yet remains. The outcome is, we are not redeemed from punishment or penalty, and, indeed, that we have no proper redemption at all on this supposition. If future punishment is a necessary remedy for a life of sin, then it in itself is a mercy, and needs no mercy to redeem from it. God's method of salvation is thus not by forgiveness through a merciful atonement, but by development and purification through a beneficent system of punishment. The result is, the atonement as a means of forgiveness is a superfluity in the divine economy. Surely a conclusion with such disastrous results to the scriptural doctrine of redemption cannot be true.

This needs to be insisted on. The Universalist, from his own premises and conclusions, admits this result, for men must undergo *all* their penalty incurred as a necessary remedy. If they undergo the penalty of sin, from what are they redeemed? From the power of sin? Well, suppose so; but then, not through Christ, but through suffering. Suffering is the great healer and restorer. But we insist that if there is any redemption from the guilt of sin, it cannot come through the endurance of the penalty. This is paying the penalty, not being delivered from it. There is no place for a true atonement on this supposition in the Restorationist's plan of salvation.*

6. Argument is attempted from certain Old Testament analogies. It is alleged that as the Jews misread the Old Testament predictions con-

---

* It is only consistent in Mr. Cox when he says: "For myself, I believe every sin must receive its due punishment" (*Salvator Mundi*, p. 227). Not only is this so of the sins of the wicked, according to this writer, but also of those of the righteous (*ibid.*, pp. 150-158).

cerning the Messiah, and, consequently, were not ready to receive him when he came, having falsely learned to look for a temporal Messiah and kingdom (for which expectation there was some ground in the apparent teaching of the older Scriptures), so we are to learn, in the matter of his second coming to judgment, not to look so much at the surface teaching of the new Scriptures, lest we make a similar mistake, but at the deeper and more " spiritual " meaning. It is suggested that as the few only perceived the real spiritual signification of the first advent, while the great body of the Jews—including priests and scribes— falsely read into the Scriptures their temporal expectation concerning the Messiah, so the "few" only to-day seem to be able to grasp the deep spiritual import of the language of the New Testament concerning the second advent. This " spiritual interpretation " is to be applied to our understanding of the language and terms that are used concerning the future punishment of the wicked. The result will be a doctrine of final universal restoration (Cox, *ut supra*, pp. 229-237). Others would gather rays of hope from such facts as the universal purpose of God in the election of the Jews, and in the laws of the first-fruits and the first-born. As the Jews were selected from among the nations, not to be the exclusive recipients of God's favors, but to be bearers of them to others (Gen. xxii, 18), and as the first-fruits were the promise and pledge of a larger ingathering, and the first-born had certain relations of helpfulness toward the later-born for which he was given a "double portion" of the inheritance, so the "elect" of Christ and the "first-fruits" and "first-born" with him have similar missions of mercy to the non-elect and larger harvest and later-born in the world's redemption, which missions are to be fulfilled, not wholly in time, or the "age" that now is, but through the "ages to come." All shall at last be saved. So slight a fact as the redemption of an ass by a lamb (Exod. xiii, 12, 13) must have its New Testament analogy, and we are to read in the fact the "eternal purpose" of God for the restoration at last of the meanest and most worthless by the ministry of the good and the pure (Jukes, *Restitution of All Things*, pp. 27–68).

As to the first analogy claimed in the interest of final universal restoration, it may be said in response: (1) The analogy would be truer if the mistake of the Jews were urged as a rebuke to the too temporal anticipations of those Christians who are looking for a thousand years' reign of Christ on the earth before the judgment. (2) The Jews were not mistaken in looking for a temporal, or earthly, kingdom of the Messiah, but in looking for the *kind* of a kingdom they expected. Christ has a temporal kingdom on earth. He reigns and rules in his Church. The Jews, through unbelief, have excluded themselves from participation in it, and from sharing for the present in its more direct privileges, although, by and by, " all Israel [that is, Israel as a people, and not in individual cases only as in the days of Paul] shall be saved " (Rom. xi, 26). (3) The word "spiritual " is not the proper word to use in the matter of plain New Testament statements concerning the lost. If the language on which the orthodox doctrine is based were wholly, or largely, figurative, the word might with some propriety be used; but not so in the case of language that is so plain and simple as it is in this case. The word " spiritual " in this connection is an unadulterated device resorted to as a convenient method to weaken the terrible force of the straightforward teaching of the divine word.

As to the other analogies urged, several remarks may be made.

1. As to the inference drawn from the election

of Israel for a world-wide mission. This mission may be aptly and appropriately urged as a lesson for the Christian Church in its mission of preaching the Gospel to every creature. Here the analogy holds good; not to an assumed mission of the saved to the unsaved in the other world. The promise, accordingly, that in Abraham's seed (Christ, Gal. iii, 16) "all the nations of the earth" should be blessed (Gen. xxii, 18), was a promise for the nations, which is being gloriously fulfilled in the Christianization of the world.

2. As to the first-born and first-fruits, it must be said, (1) If the plain teaching of the New Testament is to be any guide in our interpretation of the lessons drawn from these facts, they lend no support to the doctrine we are combating. The places where the term "first-born" is used in the New Testament are Rom. viii, 29; Col. i, 15, 18; Heb. xii, 23. In the first instance, the reference is to Christ "the first-born among many brethren;" the second, to Christ "the first-born of all creation;" the third, to him as "the first-born from the dead;" the last, to the "church of the first-born"—that is, the Church of the Hebrews. In none of these instances is there any semblance of a reference to future restoration of the lost. They, therefore, lend

no support to the doctrine. The places where the term "first-fruits" is used are Rom. viii, 23; xi, 16; xvi, 5; 1 Cor. xv, 20, 23; xvi, 15; Jas. i, 18; Rev. xiv, 4. Examination will show that in none of these instances, likewise, is there any reference to this doctrine, or the future life. (2) The doctrine of the "ages" on which this teaching is based is not tenable. If reference is made to God's "eternal purpose" (Gr. "purpose of the ages," Eph. iii, 11) for proof, we reply, The purpose here referred to is concerning the ages that are *past*, not those of the future. The verse reads, "God, according to the eternal purpose which he *purposed* in Christ Jesus our Lord." If it be said that "in the ages to come" God will "show the exceeding riches of his grace in kindness," we reply, by express limitation, toward them that are "in Christ Jesus" (Eph. ii, 7). For the rest, we refer to the fact already remarked upon, that the plural phrases containing forms of αἰών are rhetorical expressions used to intensify the thought of eternity.

II. Specific passages of Scripture used to prove the doctrine of universal restoration.

1. The first class of passages of this kind that are made to do yeoman service for this doctrine are those that exhibit the benevolent and uni-

versal provision and purpose of God concerning man's redemption. They are as follows: "For if by the trespass of the one the many died, much more did the grace of God, and the gift by the grace of the one man, Jesus Christ, abound unto the many" (Rom. v, 15). "So then as through one trespass the judgment came unto all men to condemnation; even so through one act of righteousness the free gift came unto all men to justification of life" (*ibid.*, verse 18; compare the whole passage, 12–21). "But all things are of God, who reconciled us to himself through Christ, and gave unto us the ministry of reconciliation; to wit, that God was in Christ reconciling the world unto himself, not reckoning unto them their trespasses, and having committed unto us the word of reconciliation" (2 Cor. v. 18, 19). "Behold, the Lamb of God, which taketh away the sin of the world!" (John i, 29). "And we have beheld and bear witness that the Father hath sent the Son to be the Saviour of the world" (1 John iv, 14), etc.

Concerning these passages it will be sufficient to reply, with Müller, that they "cannot be made to sanction the idea of universal restoration, unless we adopt the principle that the final issue of the divine purposes must coincide with their primary tendency and design; in other words, that God could not arrange his purposes according to the free action of man in relation to them" (*Christian Doctrine of Sin*, vol. ii, p. 426); adding, simply, that they are to be " studied in their connection," and according to the "analogy of faith." According to this last hermeneutical law, as general statements they are to be limited by other limiting passages of the divine word, as, for example, those which declare the conditions of their fulfillment or realization. These limiting conditions are not doubtful. " Except ye repent ye shall all in like manner perish" (Luke xiii, 3). " That whosoever believeth may in him have eternal life" (John iii, 15). " Except ye eat the flesh of the Son of man and drink his blood, ye have not life in yourselves" (John vi, 53), etc.

2. Another set of passages that are used to prove this doctrine concern the resurrection of the dead and the " consummation of the world " (συντέλεια τοῦ αἰῶνος). Chief among these are: " For as in Adam all die, so also in Christ shall all be made alive" (1 Cor. xv, 22). " For he must reign, till he hath put all his enemies under his feet. The last enemy that shall be abolished is death" (*ibid.*, verses 25, 26). " And when all

things have been subjected unto him, then shall the Son also himself be subjected to him that did subject all things unto him, that God may be all in all" (*ibid.*, verse 28; compare the entire passage, 20–28). "Whom the heaven must receive until the times of restoration [Authorized Version, "restitution"] of all things, whereof God spake by the mouth of his holy prophets which have been since the world began" (Acts iii, 21). These passages demand separate treatment.

"For as in Adam all die, so also in Christ shall all be made alive." These words are similar to much of the language in the fifth of Romans, the one having reference to physical death and resurrection, the other to moral or spiritual. The emphasis which writers of this class lay upon them is the same in both cases. Consequently, the observations made upon the passages in Romans will equally apply here (p. 92). It is necessary to add further, simply, that the apostle, in the entire chapter, is writing to Christian believers concerning the reality of the resurrection. There had grown up in the Church at Corinth some doubt as to this doctrine, and Paul would re-establish and confirm their faith in it. He does not attempt to prove the universality of the resurrection, but simply seeks to establish the *fact* of the resurrection. His particular thought was with reference to the resurrection of the righteous dead (witness this in the general drift of the whole chapter, and in such particular statements as in verses 51, 52, 58), as was his thought in writing of the same doctrine, from other reasons, to the Thessalonians (1 Thess. iv, 13-18); and, proving the fact of the resurrection, he asserts that, "as in Adam all [meaning the righteous] die, so also in Christ shall all [the righteous] be made alive." And at all events, there is no ground in these words for asserting the doctrine of universal restoration; for other Scriptures which teach the universality of the resurrection teach also that the issue is a twofold result—some are raised to "life," and others are raised to condemnation. " Marvel not at this: for the hour cometh, in which all that are in the tombs shall hear his voice, and shall come forth ; they that have done good, unto the resurrection of life; and they that have done ill, unto the resurrection of judgment " (John v, 28, 29.* Compare Dan. xii, 2).

---

* It is useless to try to prove that our Lord in this case was speaking of a spiritual, or moral, resurrection ; for, if so, wherein is the difference between those raised to "life" and those raised to "judgment?" Also, the phrase "marvel not at this" marks a change of thought from the moral resurrection spoken of in

"For he must reign, till he hath put all his enemies under his feet. The last enemy that shall be abolished is death." The facts involved in this text and its connections have already been referred to in our proofs of the doctrine of future punishment. We refer to them again in this connection because Universalists lay so much stress upon the passage given to prove their doctrine. They are as follows: The end of the mediatorial reign of Christ accompanies the destruction of the "last enemy," and the last enemy that is to be destroyed is physical death, in and by the resurrection, leaving the "æonian punishment," pronounced at the judgment, to follow this destruction of the *last* enemy.

There is not the shadow of a reason for the statement in Martensen, that when Paul says "'the last enemy that shall be destroyed is death'" —therefore the other, the second death; because otherwise there would still remain an un-

---

verse 25, and that in the verses we are considering. Our Lord's hearers were exhorted not to marvel at the soul resurrection from the death of sin, because the time would come when even the bodies of men would be raised from the tomb. Again, the difference in the two cases is shown by the two phrases, "the hour cometh, and now is," in the first case, and simply "the hour cometh," in the second—the one was present, the other future. Besides, it is forced and artificial to identify the "dead" of the first instance with "all that are in tombs" of the second.

conquerable enemy" (*Christian Dogmatics*, p. 475). The fact is in proof of the very reverse of this, as we have seen. The argument of Martensen, moreover, is a clear case of *potitio principii*. His assertion is to the effect that all men are to be restored because Paul says the "last enemy to be destroyed is death," and that Paul's expression includes the "second death" because otherwise all men would not be restored. We are willing that the Universalist shall have all the defense he can get from this sort of logic. We know his need of it.

But to reiterate for the sake of emphasis, the order of events at the consummation of the world (Matt. xxviii, 20) is as follows: (1) The parousia, or coming of Christ; (2) the resurrection of the dead; (3) the judgment; (4) the end of Christ's mediatorial reign, when the kingdom will be delivered up to the Father. These events occur at the same time, or in immediate succession.* The wicked, therefore,

---

* No account is taken here of the millennium, for in any case the order of events is the same; and the general resurrection, when the last enemy is to be destroyed, follows the parousia (however long or short the interval), and comes before the judgment. The significance of the πρώτη ἀνάστασις, and other facts and difficulties connected with the millennium, do not enter, therefore, for consideration here.

are to go away into æonian punishment after, or at the consummation, of all things. There remains, therefore, for them no more hope. Their judgment to death is part of the consummation of all things.

"And when all things have been subjected unto him, then shall the Son also himself be subjected to him that did subject all things unto him, that God may be all in all." The most that is said in this passage is that all things shall be subjected unto Christ, and, finally, Christ to God. There is nothing in this statement to lend the least support to the doctrine of universal restoration.

Much is made of the phrase, "that God may be all in all." One writer comments thus: "'That God may be,' not all in some, but 'all in all.'" Nothing could show the perversity of the interpretation of writers of this class better than this. Not only is the whole context ignored, as is oftenest the case with these writers, but the manifest meaning of "divine supremacy" is also overlooked. The words do not mean that God may be all in all persons, but simply that he may be supreme. (Compare Eph. i, 23.)

"Whom the heaven must receive until the times of restoration of all things, whereof God spake by the mouth of his holy prophets which have been since the world began." As is well known, it is this text that furnishes the often-used and, exegetically, much-abused phrase, ἀποκατάστασις πάντων—"restitution of all things." This phrase has come to be used by some writers as synonomous with universal restoration. Its abuse will be seen when it is remembered that there is good ground for the assertion that the word αποκατάστασις does not mean restitution or restoration in this place, in any proper sense of the word, at all, but "fulfillment," having reference to the fulfillment "of all things, whereof [or which, ὧν] God spake by the mouth of his holy prophets since the world began." (Compare Matt. xvii, 11.) But if the word be accepted to mean "restitution" or "restoration," that it cannot include the idea of the final universal restoration of the lost is manifest from the following fact, namely, that "the times of the restoration of all things" are to be fulfilled at the coming of our Lord. "The heaven must receive" him "until" then. The "restoration of all things" precedes, therefore, the εἰς τοὺς αἰῶνας τῶν αἰώνων of future punishment. Besides, the "prophets" have nowhere spoken of universal restoration.

3. Still another class of passages that are urged in favor of universal restoration are those that

speak of the "reconciliation" or summing up of all things in Christ, whether they be things in heaven or things on earth. The two most explicit passages of this class are Eph. i, 9, 10, and Col. i, 19, 20. They are as follows: "Having made known unto us the mystery of his will, according to his good pleasure which he purposed in him unto a dispensation of the fullness of the times, to sum up all things in Christ [ἀνακεφαλαιώσασθαι τὰ πάντα ἐν τῷ Χριστῷ], the things in the heavens, and the things upon the earth." "For it was the good pleasure of the Father that in him should all the fullness dwell; and through him to reconcile all things unto himself, having made peace through the blood of his cross; through him, I say, whether things upon the earth, or things in the heavens."

We gladly recognize the deep and glorious truth of these words. Christ is a cosmic Being, having a universal relation to all things, both in the heavens and on the earth. Just what that relation to other worlds than ours is, except that it must be beneficent, we cannot know. The two words used in the above quoted passages (ἀνακεφαλαιόω, ἀποκαταλλάσσω) furnish us with a general statement of some beneficent relation to the heavens as well as to the earth; but just what we, perhaps, in its fullness, will never know. There is no reason for supposing that the efficacy of the cross, except in its moral lesson to other intelligences, extends beyond our own world, since it was wrought on earth and in our nature ; and just what the special implication of the reconciliation and re-heading, or summing up, of all things "in the heavens" may be, we cannot know. Our reconciliation to God is through the sacrifice of the cross; how and in what sense * that of the heavens is effected we are not told. The same remark is to be made concerning the summing up of all things in the heavens in Christ, since this is most likely the same as the reconciliation ; or, at least, the one is involved in the other.

But whatever the significance of this reconcil-

---

* The reconciliation of things on earth is distincily said to be "peace through the blood of his cross." This divine and gracious work seems to be separate in the thought of the text from the undefined and general reconciliation of all things in heaven and on earth. The reconciliation on earth seems separately and specially given—"having made peace," etc.—the other is not. Besides, if we assume that other worlds are reconciled, as is ours, by the death of the cross, we must assume universal sinfulness in the universe ; for our reconciliation is through an infinite sacrifice on account of sin. But some, at least, of the angels we know have not sinned. This is involved in the expression in Jude 6, "The angels which kept not their own principality, but left their proper habitation," etc. Some did keep "their own principality." Still further, that our atonement is not for the angels is emphatically involved in Heb. ii, 16.

iation and summing up of all things in Christ may be, and the specific agency of their realization, these texts can lend no support to the doctrine we are opposing. One manifest reason is, that they say nothing about it. Another is, that they limit the reconciliation to the things in the heavens and on the earth. The comment of Dr. Jukes is evidently coined for the emergency: "'Whether they be things in heaven'—that is, the spirit-world, where the conflict with Satan yet is—'or things on earth'—that is, this outward world, where death now reigns, and where even God's elect are by nature children of wrath, even as other men" * (*ut supra*, p. 22).

But we insist upon it, if the doctrine of universal restoration is true, that the great apostle did not say, "And things under the earth," in these passages, is not to be accounted for. What a magnificent opportunity Paul had to teach this doctrine had he so desired, and how natural it would have been to do so if it were true! The limitation seems intentional when

---

* The unreliableness of this writer as an exegete is demonstrated in the turn of thought he gives to the passage referred to in the latter part of the quotation, as in many other instances. In this case Dr. Jukes says: "Where even God's elect *are* by nature children of wrath," etc.; whereas Paul says, "*were* by nature children of wrath."

we consider the fact that this apostle in other connections, and where the thought is of universal subjugation to Christ, without specifying whether it is voluntary or compulsory (Phil. ii, 9, 10*), uses the very phrase, "and things under the earth." As Paul was familiar with the fact that "every knee" in heaven and earth and hell should bow to Christ, why, we urge, did he not say "and things under the earth" when speaking of the re-heading and reconciliation of all things in Christ if the Universalist is right? The conclusion is patent and inevitable. Paul, who had already declared that the wicked "shall suffer punishment, even eternal destruction from the face of the Lord and from the glory of his might" (2 Thess. i, 9), knew that for the lost there was "no more a sacrifice for sins" (Heb. x, 26).

4. Still another class of passages that are used by the Universalist to support his claim are some that relate to the universal conquest of the Gospel, or that show the world-wide mission of

---

* That the thought in this text implies the universal supremacy of Christ and his kingdom, without specifying what is the character of the subjection, is manifest to all but those who insist on reading their doctrine of restoration into it. Bowing the knee was an act of homage and subjection for both friendly and unfriendly subjects. Moreover, the phrase is used in Rom. xiv, 10–12, with special reference to the "judgment." (Compare Eph. iii, 14; Matt. xxvii, 29; Isa. xlv, 23.)

Christianity. Of course, the Universalist will not allow the claim involved in this classification; but a slight examination, in most instances, will show the validity of it.

The chief passages of this class are as follows: "And in thy seed shall all the nations of the earth be blessed" (Gen. xxii, 18). "And so all Israel shall be saved" (Rom. xi, 26). "Who willeth that all men should be saved, and come to the knowledge of the truth. For there is one God, one Mediator also between God and men, himself man, Christ Jesus, who gave himself a ransom for all; the testimony to be borne in its own times" (1 Tim. ii, 4–6). "And I, if I be lifted up from the earth, will draw all men unto myself" (John xii, 32).

The first two passages have already been referred to in the course of this discussion, and need but a moment's consideration here. That the promise to Abraham, that in his seed the world should be blessed, was a promise which had reference to the universal spread of Christianity, may be proved by the fact that it concerned the "nations," and that Paul so applies it (Gal. iii, 8). That that referring to the salvation of "all Israel" is to be understood as referring to the conversion of the Jews as a people to Christianity may be proved by reference to the entire passage in which the words occur (Rom. xi). Here it will be found that the apostle is contrasting and explaining the conversion of the Gentiles and the rejection of Israel; not every individual Israelite, but Israel as a people. A "remnant" had already been saved, "according to the election of grace" (verse 5), by faith; but Israel as a people had been "broken off" through unbelief (verse 20). Paul, however, foresees the time when "all Israel shall be saved," or when Israel as a people shall be restored to the covenanted privileges from which they had excluded themselves.

The reference of the other two passages is likewise unmistakable. That the passage in First Timothy refers to the conversion of the world will be seen by including the seventh verse: " Whereunto I was appointed a preacher and an apostle (I speak the truth, I lie not), a teacher of the Gentiles in faith and truth." Paul's reference in this verse to the Gentiles shows the universal thought he has of the Gospel when he says Christ was given "a ransom for all; the testimony to be borne in its own times." The whole context (verses 1-8) is helpful to the same exposition. The import of John xii, 32, may be judged from the explicit reference of verse 31: "Now is the judgment of this world: now shall the prince of this world be cast out," preceding immediately the words of the text. The occasion also shows beyond any doubt what thought our Lord had in mind when he uttered the words. Certain Greeks (Gentiles) had come to see him. This gives rise to a discourse by Christ, the leading thought of which is, as Tholuck expresses it, "in the longing of these Gentiles is an anticipation of the future conversion of the world." The "all men," then, of this passage is synonomous with the "all nations" of Gen. xxii, 18, and the "all" of 1 Tim. ii, 4-6.

5. Two passages of Scripture urged in favor of this doctrine, that form a class by themselves, are Matt. v, 26: "Verily I say unto thee, Thou shalt by no means come out thence, till thou have paid the last farthing;" and Luke xii, 47, 48: "And that servant, which knew his lord's will, and made not ready, nor did according to his will, shall be beaten with many stripes; but he that knew not, and did things worthy of stripes, shall be beaten with few stripes." It is affirmed that both of these passages involve the cessation of punishment.

It is to be said: (1) If they teach the cessation

of punishment in the cases to which they refer, they would not, therefore, teach *universal* restoration. The most, in any case, that can be claimed from them is that they teach the restoration of *some*. We would then have both "eternal" and "temporal" future punishment. (2) But it is to be questioned whether the first passage (as, perhaps, Matt. xii, 32) expresses more than an "emphasized negative" in relation to the condition of the lost. (3) The second passage can be explained, after the common fashion, to signify *degrees* in punishment rather than duration. It is confessedly a figurative mode of speech, and can, therefore, teach nothing that contradicts other and explicit declarations of the divine word.

6. Miscellaneous. There are a few other passages that need brief consideration that cannot be otherwise classified than as miscellaneous. These are: "For God hath shut up all unto disobedience, that he might have mercy upon all" (Rom. xi, 32); "For to this end Christ died, and lived again, that he might be Lord of both the dead and the living" (Rom. xiv, 9); "For to this end we labor and strive, because we have our hope set on the living God, who is the Saviour of all men, specially of them that believe" (1 Tim. iv, 10); "And death and Hades were cast

into the lake of fire" (Rev. xx, 14); "And he shall wipe away every tear from their eyes; and death shall be no more; neither shall there be mourning, nor crying, nor pain, any more: the first things are passed away. And he that sitteth on the throne said, Behold, I make all things new" (Rev. xxi, 4, 5); "And there shall be no curse any more" (Rev. xxii, 3). We will consider these in the order given.

"For God hath shut up all unto disobedience, that he might have mercy upon all." The import of this verse is no doubt identical with that of Rom. iii, 9: "For we before laid to the charge both of Jews and Greeks, that they are all under sin," and Gal. iii, 22: "Howbeit the Scripture hath shut up all things under sin, that the promise by faith in Jesus Christ might be given to them that believe." This last passage distinctly limits the "promise by faith in Jesus Christ" to "them that believe." This is in keeping with the whole teaching of Romans (for example, iii, 21, 22) and the other Scriptures, and must be understood here.

"For to this end Christ died, and lived again, that he might be Lord of both the dead and the living." The apostle is teaching the duty of the strong toward the weak, particularly in the matter of eating meat and observing days. He asserts: "He that regardeth the day, regardeth it unto the Lord: and he that eateth, eateth unto the Lord, for he giveth God thanks; and he that eateth not, unto the Lord he eateth not, and giveth God thanks. For none of us liveth to himself, and none dieth to himself. For whether we live, we live unto the Lord; or whether we die, we die unto the Lord: whether we live therefore, or die, we are the Lord's" (verses 6-8). And then follows immediately upon this the verse we are considering. The connections clearly show that the lordship of Christ over the dead and the living is confined by the apostle's thought in this passage to believers; not that it is intentionally so confined, but because Paul had no occasion to think of any others. "Whether *we* live, *we* live unto the Lord; or whether *we* die, *we* die unto the Lord: whether *we* live therefore, or die, *we* are the Lord's." Christ both "died, and lived again," that he might be Lord of his own, dead and alive. "Thus it is," as Godet says, "that he reigns simultaneously over the two domains of being through which his own are called to pass, and that he can fulfill his promise to them (John x, 28): 'None shall pluck them out of my hand'" (Commentary, *in loco*). The Universalist, therefore, can find in this passage no valid ground for his doctrine.

" For to this end we labor and strive, because we have our hope set on the living God, who is the Saviour of all men, specially of them that believe." As to this passage it is only necessary to say that if Paul is to be interpreted by himself the two phrases, " Saviour of all men" and "specially of them that believe," can have no doubtful meaning. The first is illustrated by such passages as the following : " Even so through one act of righteousness the free gift came unto all men to justification of life" (Rom. v, 18); " For the love of Christ constraineth us ; because we thus judge, that one died for all, therefore all died; and he died for all, that they which live should no longer live unto themselves, but unto him who for their sakes died and rose again " (2 Cor. v, 14, 15); the second, by these : " For I am not ashamed of the gospel : for it is the power of God unto salvation to every one that believeth; to the Jew first, and also to the Greek " (Rom. i, 16); " By their unbelief they were broken off, and thou standest by thy faith " (Rom. xi, 20). Christ is the Saviour of all men— this the Scriptures every-where gloriously reveal; but he is also " specially " (μάλιστα—" in the greatest degree"—that is, in "the greatest and fullest exhibition of his σωτηρια, its complete realization") the Saviour "of them that believe." This is so here and hereafter. Christ is the Saviour of all in his provisions of mercy and grace ; of those that believe, in the full realization of those provisions in a saved experience.

"And death and Hades were cast into the lake of fire." It is said this involves the destruction of death and Hades. The inference is, "Therefore the second death and Gehenna ;" this latter from the fact that Hades, or the under world, includes Gehenna.

It will be sufficient to refute this argument to refer to the verse immediately following the one for which so much is claimed. After saying death and Hades were cast into the lake of fire, John says : " And if any was not found written in the book of life, he was cast into the lake of fire" (verse 15). It is unfortunate for the Universalist that he cannot find a second "lake of fire" into which this first one is cast ; and if so it would not involve the restoration of those cast into it.

Attempted arguments like the above simply increase one's wonder at the manifest unfairness of the exposition of the Scriptures by which the doctrine of restoration is sought to be established.

The last two passages may be considered together. "And he shall wipe away every tear from their eyes; and death shall be no more; neither shall there be mourning, nor crying, nor pain, any more: the first things are passed away. And he that sitteth on the throne said, Behold, I make all things new." "And there shall be no curse any more." If the reader will examine the passages in their connections he will find in both cases that after them in the same chapter there is distinct reference to another state of things for the wicked. In the first case, in chapter xxi, 8, we have, "But for the fearful, and unbelieving, and abominable, and murderers, and fornicators, and sorcerers, and idolaters, and all liars, their part shall be in the lake that burneth with fire and brimstone; which is the second death." In the second case, in the twenty-second chapter and the fifteenth verse, we have, "Without are the dogs, and the sorcerers, and the fornicators, and the murderers, and the idolaters, and every one that loveth and maketh a lie." From these facts it must appear to all that the passages cited furnish no support for the doctrine of restoration. But if examination is made again it will be found that these things are said by explicit reference to the righteous. "He that overcometh shall inherit these things" (xxi, 7). In the same verse with the second of the two passages is this: "And his servants shall do him service," and following this in the next verse: "And they shall see his face; and his name shall be on their foreheads."

We have now completed a brief survey of the leading objections and arguments of the Universalists. We have not consciously omitted reference to any important fact or consideration; but, on the other hand, we have endeavored to deal fairly with the doctrine we oppose in every case, a hundred times wishing that we might find in the arguments of its advocates some valid ground for faith in it to rest upon. To use a common but apt figure, again and again, like the dove of the ark, we have wandered over the waste of biblical criticism on this subject, seeking some place to rest our feet in confidence; but after repeated and vain research we have had to return, on exegetical grounds, to the old ark of the orthodox Church, and believe her teaching to be that only which will bear the test of the Scriptures. For no "larger hope" can we desert this stronghold of the truth; and in this confidence it shall be our aim, whether our pleasure or not (Jon. iii, 2), to persuade men to "flee from the wrath to come" (Matt. iii, 7).

"And if any man shall take away from the words of the book of this prophecy, God shall take away his part out of the book of life, and out of the holy city, and from the things which are written in this book."—Rev. xxii, 19.

CHAPTER III.

New Testament Terminology Respecting Future Retribution.

IT is not our conviction that the words of the Bible in either their classical or Jewish signification, or in themselves, considered in an isolated fashion and alone, can at all determine the question of the future life. Their biblical signification is rather to be determined by the general scope and spirit of the passages in which they are found, and by the whole teaching of the Scriptures on the subject by all the proof adduced in the first chapter of this book. Remembering these qualifications, however, a study of the subject from the present stand-point will not be without its results, and seems necessary to a full understanding of all the facts in the case.

The terms that demand attention may be classified and treated as follows: 1. Those that pertain to the place of future punishment, ᾅδης —Hades (Heb. שְׁאוֹל); γέεννα—Gehenna; ταρταρώσας—Tartarus; φρέαρ, ἄβυσσος, λίμνη τοῦ πυρός. 2. Those that pertain to time, or the duration of punishment, αἰων (with its plural forms and phrases), αἰώνιος, ἀίδιος. 3. Those that describe the condition or state of the lost, θάνατος, ἀπώλεια, ἀπόλλυμι, ὄλεθρος, ἐξολοθρεύω, διαφθείρω, ἀποκτείνω, φθορά, ἀφανίζω, etc. This we believe to be an exhaustive classification of the more important terms used in connection with the subject, and in this order we will briefly consider them.*

1. Those that pertain to the place of future punishment. Three of these, ᾅδης, γέεννα, ταρταρώσας, are in all instances alike translated in the Authorized Version (two of them, γέεννα, ταρταρώσας, in the Revised, with an additional marginal reading) by the English word "hell." These we will consider first in their order, and follow with a short account of the remaining words.

῞Αιδης, translated "hell" in the Authorized Version and "Hades" in the Revised in every in-

---

* We omit reference here to the words κρίνω, κατακρίνω, κρίμα, κρίσις (translated "to damn" and "damnation" in the Authorized Version, but, rightly, "judged" [2 Thess. ii, 12], "condemned" [Mark xvi, 16], "condemnation" [Mark xii, 40], "judgment" [Matt. xxiii, 33] in the Revised), because in the nature of the case their signification is very general, and they therefore express nothing definite either as to the duration or the character of future punishment. In the phrase "judgment of hell" (Greek Gehenna), for example, the word that conveys a definite meaning is "hell," not κρίσις.

stance,* is derived, according to etymologists, from ἀ privative and ἰδεῖν, to see, signifying that which is not seen. It is used in the Septuagint in translating the Hebrew שְׁאוֹל in most instances, a word with which it is identical in several particulars. In the Greek writings (always in Homer) it is used as the name of Pluto or Dis, the god of the spirit-world. It was also used in these writings to signify the spirit-world itself. In later Greek this became its more common meaning. In the New Testament it is undoubtedly identical in meaning with the secondary classical signification, except that in classic usage it was understood to signify the permanent abode of the dead, whereas in the New Testament it signifies the abode of the dead before the resurrection (Rev. xx, 14). In two instances it is personified as a living power (Rev. vi, 8; xx, 14). In other instances it has a metaphorical signification (Matt. xi, 23; Luke x, 15). There can be no doubt, moreover, that it was used to represent the after-death abode of the righteous and the unrighteous alike (Luke xvi, 23; compare Acts ii, 27, 31). In this respect it was kindred in its

---

*In 1 Cor. xv, 55 (where in the Authorized Version we have "grave," ᾅδης), θάνατος is substituted for ᾅδης, according to the best manuscripts, and is so given in the Revised Version.

use to that of the Greek and Latin writers, who divided Hades into Tartarus for the bad and Elysium for the good. But it seems equally certain that it was used sometimes as equivalent simply to the abode of wicked spirits (Matt. xvi, 18). It is on this supposition, moreover, that the metaphorical use of the word in Matt. xi, 23, and Luke x, 15, can have any significance. In both this latter respect and the one preceding it is the same as the Hebrew שְׁאוֹל (Gen. xlii, 38; Psa. ix, 17; Psa. cxxxix, 8; Prov. ix, 18). In all general respects the usage was the same in the Jewish and early Christian writings outside of the Scriptures.*

As to the common impressions that prevailed concerning this unseen world, a remark or two may be made. In both classic and Jewish writings it was thought of as being in the earth, or under it, according to the false astronomy of the times; and the grave was supposed to be the entrance into it. As Christ did not come to

---

* Later, however, the fathers located Paradise (the place of the righteous dead) elsewhere than in Hades. " Origen placed it in an apartment of heaven—the third heaven. More and more the feeling spread, especially after Origen's time, that Hades, the under-world, was a gloomy, undesirable region, where there could be nothing but suffering, and where Satan held sway" (*Discussions in History and Theology*, G. P. Fisher, p. 417).

teach science, he, together with the writers of the New Testament, used the common forms of thought and expression in the matter as he found them. The Old Testament idea of this world seems to have been that of a shadowy and somewhat dismal abode even for the righteous (Psa. vi, 5; Job x, 21, 22). Its expressions concerning it were vague and uncertain. Unlike this was Hades to the heathen writers. "The pagan poets gave the popular mind definite pictures of Tartarus and Elysium; of Styx and Acheron; of happy plains where dead heroes held high discourse, and of black abysses where offenders underwent strange and ingenious tortures." The New Testament idea was more definite, and more cheerful for the good. It was divided into Paradise, or Abraham's bosom (the Jews also spoke of it as the "Garden of Eden" and the "Tree of Life"—Edersheim), for the righteous, and Gehenna for the wicked. It is thought by some writers that the New Testament represents the saints since the resurrection as going immediately upon death to heaven. There certainly seems, in some instances at least, to be a changed attitude and expression toward the other life. Witness, for example, the case of Stephen when stoned (Acts vii, 55, 56, 59. Compare Phil. i, 21, 23, etc.; but see also p. 127).

The passages in the New Testament where the word ᾅδης is given are as follows: "And thou, Capernaum, shalt thou be exalted unto heaven? thou shalt go down unto Hades: for if the mighty works had been done in Sodom which were done in thee, it would have remained until this day" (Matt. xi, 23); "And I also say unto thee, that thou art Peter, and upon this rock I will build my church; and the gates of Hades shall not prevail against it" (Matt. xvi, 18); "And thou, Capernaum, shalt thou be exalted unto heaven? thou shalt be brought down unto Hades" (Luke x, 15); "And in Hades he lifted up his eyes, being in torments, and seeth Abraham afar off, and Lazarus in his bosom" (Luke xvi, 23); "Because thou wilt not leave my soul in Hades, neither wilt thou give thy Holy One to see corruption." "He foreseeing this spake of the resurrection of the Christ, that neither was he left in Hades, nor did his flesh see corruption" (Acts ii, 27, 31); "And I was dead, and behold, I am alive for evermore, and I have the keys of death and of Hades" (Rev. i, 18); "And I saw, and behold, a pale horse: and he that sat upon him, his name was death;

and Hades followed with him" (Rev. vi, 8); "And the sea gave up the dead which were in it; and death and Hades gave up the dead which were in them: and they were judged every man according to their works. And death and Hades were cast into the lake of fire" (Rev. xx, 13, 14).

Γέεννα. This word is the Grecized form of the Hebrew גֵּי הִנֹּם, valley of Hinnom—or more fully גֵּיא בֶּן־הִנֹּם, or גֵּי בְנֵי־הִנֹּם. The etymology of the word הִנֹּם is uncertain. Some suppose it is the name of a man. Others think it is derived from a root signifying "lamentation," in reference to the cry of the children offered in sacrifice to Molech in the valley of its name.

This valley (also called Tophet, most probably from the root תּוּף, "to spit upon," hence "abhorred") was on the south and west of Jerusalem. It is first mentioned in the Scriptures in Josh. xv, 8; xviii, 16, in connection with the description of the boundaries of the territories of Judah and Benjamin. In the time of Solomon the worship of Molech—a bull-shaped image into whose burning arms the Jews learned to cast their children—was set up in it (1 Kings xi, 7), and Ahaz set the example for the people of making his own "son to pass through the fire, according to the abominations of the heathen" (2 Kings xvi, 3). These rites continued to be practiced until the time of Josiah, who "defiled" the place and overthrew the heathenish worship (2 Kings xxiii, 10). On account of the horrible rites there practiced the Jews afterward made the valley the common place of sewage for the filth of the city. The carcasses of animals and the bodies of criminals were also thrown into it. A fire was kept burning in it for the purpose of destroying these things and to prevent pestilence. These facts made the place afterward to be looked upon as a symbol of the place of future punishment. Hence "Gehenna" became the name of the place of the lost in Hades, and was so used by the Jews in the time of Christ.

The term γέεννα is used in the New Testament twelve times, in every instance but one (Jas. iii, 6) in the gospels. Twice it is used in the phrase γέεννα τοῦ πυρός—"Gehenna of fire" (Matt. v, 22; xviii, 9). Once we have υἱὸς γεέννης —"son of Gehenna" (Matt. xxiii, 15)—and once κρίσις τῆς γεέννης—"judgment of Gehenna" (Matt. xxiii, 33).

The passages in which the word is found are as follows: "But I say unto you, that every one who is angry with his brother shall be in danger of the judgment; and whosoever shall say to his brother, Raca, shall be in danger of the council; and whosoever shall say, Thou fool, shall be in danger of the hell of fire" (Matt. v, 22); "And if thy right eye causeth thee to stumble, pluck it out, and cast it from thee: for it is profitable for thee that one of thy members should perish, and not thy whole body be cast into hell. And if thy right hand causeth thee to stumble, cut it off, and cast it from thee: for it is profitable for thee that one of thy members should perish, and not thy whole body go into hell" (Matt. v, 29, 30); "And be not afraid of them which kill the body, but are not able to kill the soul: but rather fear him which is able to destroy both soul and body in hell" (Matt. x, 28); "And if thine eye causeth thee to stumble, pluck it out, and cast it from thee: it is good for thee to enter into life with one eye, rather than having two eyes to be cast into the hell of fire" (Matt. xviii, 9); "Woe unto you, scribes and Pharisees, hypocrites! for ye compass sea and land to make one proselyte; and when he is become so, ye make him twofold more a son of hell than yourselves" (Matt. xxiii, 15); "Ye serpents, ye offspring of vipers, how shall ye escape the judgment of hell?" (Matt. xxiii, 33); "And if thy hand cause thee to stumble, cut it off: it is good for thee to enter into life maimed, rather than having thy two hands to go into hell, into the unquenchable fire. And if thy foot cause thee to stumble, cut it off: it is good for thee to enter into life halt, rather than having thy two feet to be cast into hell. And if thine eye cause thee to stumble, cast it out: it is good for thee to enter into the kingdom of God with one eye, rather than having two eyes to be cast into hell; where their worm dieth not, and the fire is not quenched" (Mark ix, 43, 45, 47); "But I will warn you whom ye shall fear: Fear him, which after he hath killed hath power to cast into hell; yea, I say unto you, Fear him" (Luke xii, 5); "And the tongue is a fire: the world of iniquity among our members is the tongue, which defileth the whole body, and setteth on fire the wheel of nature, and is set on fire by hell" (Jas. iii, 6).

Ταρταρώσας. This word is found but once in the Bible (2 Pet. ii, 4), and is translated "hell" in both versions. It is the aorist participle of the verb ταρταρόω—"to hurl into Tartarus"—and is used as a noun for τάρταρος—Tartarus.

Τάρταρος signified to the Greeks in their older

writings a place below Hades as far as the latter was below heaven. This was the prison of the Titans, and the place into which Zeus threw "the worst offenders against his authority." In the later writers it was used to signify the underworld in general (hence synonomous with Hades), and, particularly, as one part of Hades, the abode of wicked spirits, as over against Elysium, the place of the good (Liddell and Scott). It was used chiefly in this latter signification.

The passage in Peter in which the word is found reads as follows: " For if God spared not angels when they sinned, but cast them down to hell, and committed them to pits of darkness, to be reserved unto judgment: . . . the Lord knoweth how to deliver the godly out of temptation, and to keep the unrighteous under punishment unto the day of judgment."

When it is remembered that for the incurably wicked the Greeks knew no restoration from Tartarus, the intent of the apostle in using the word in this passage cannot be doubtful.

If it is objected that Peter expressly limits the state of things described in the passage to the time of "judgment," in response we would refer the reader to the fact already given, that wicked men and devils are to suffer an æonian punishment after the judgment. Granting, therefore, that the passage here teaches a punishment to last only until the judgment, the other passages referred to settle the question of punishment after that event.

Φρέαρ, ἄβυσσος, λίμνη τοῦ πυρός. These words may be considered together. The first is used seven times in the New Testament, three times translated "well" (Luke xiv, 5 [in A. V. "pit"]; John iv, 11, 12), four times (Rev. ix, 1, 2), "pit." In this latter connection it is used twice with ἄβυσσος, and is translated in the Revised Version "the pit of the abyss." In the four places in Revelation it seems to be identical in signification with Gehenna and Tartarus in Hades. Ἄβυσσος—"abyss"—is in Rom. x, 7, and Rev. ix, 1, 2, used of the under-world in general. In the first case reference is made to Christ's descent into Hades. In Rev. ix, 1, 2, the "pit" is *in* the abyss. In other places it seems to signify simply Gehenna, Tartarus, or the "pit." The demons of Luke viii, 31, requested that they might not be sent into the "abyss" (ἄβυσσος). So, also, Rev. ix, 11; xi, 7; xvii, 8; xx, 1, 3. The phrase λίμνη τοῦ πυρός—"lake of fire"—is found only in Revelation, and in every case signifies the place of future punishment. In one case the phrase is "lake of fire and brimstone" —θειον—(chap. xx, 10); in another, "the lake that burneth with fire and brimstone" (chap. xxi, 8); once, "the lake of fire that burneth with brimstone" (chap. xix, 20). Twice the "lake of fire" is identified with the "second death" (chap. xx, 14; xxi, 8). From Rev. xx, 14, "and death and Hades were cast into the lake of fire," we might infer that "the lake of fire" is meant to signify the place of the κόλασις αἰώνιος after the judgment, Hades as the place of the righteous and unrighteous dead alike no longer existing, the "world" and the saved having been "perfected," or consummated (Matt. xxviii, 20; Phil. i, 6).

2. The second class of terms, as we have named them, are those that pertain to the duration of future punishment.

First among these is αἰών. The most generally received etymology connects this word with ἀεί (always), and makes it identical with the Latin *ævum*, from which we get the English aye or ever, deriving Greek, Latin, and English ultimately from the Sanskrit *évas*. The significations of the word are not doubtful either in the classics or the Scriptures. In the former the word signifies "an age," "human life time," "life itself;" also, "an unbroken age, perpetuity of time, eternity." With its classic usage corresponds in some particulars its use in the Septuagint (in translating the Hebrew עוֹלָם) and in the New Testament. In both of these, however, it has significations peculiar to themselves. We are concerned chiefly with the use of the word in the New Testament. Here it signifies:

(1) An age. In this sense it is used to signify a dispensation, or economy. The Jews were in the habit of dividing time into two periods, that which preceded the Messiah (הָעוֹלָם הַזֶּה), and that which would be after his advent (הָעוֹלָם הַבָּא). The New Testament writers adopted the same division of time, and in a number of instances referred to the present age preceding the parousia as ὁ αἰὼν οὗτος—this age (Rom. xii, 2), ὁ αἰών—the age (Matt. xiii, 22), ὁ ἐνεστὼς αἰών—the present, or existing age (Gal. i, 4), ὁ νῦν αἰών—the now age (1 Tim. vi, 17); to that which will succeed the parousia as αἰὼν μέλλων—the future age (Matt. xii, 32), ὁ αἰὼν ἐκεῖνος—that age (Luke xx, 35), ὁ αἰὼν ὁ ἐρχόμενος—the coming age (Luke xviii, 30). In some instances the word seems synonomous with "the time of life," or, at least, it involves this idea. Hence Demas is

condemned for having loved "the now age"—
ἀγαπήσας τὸν νῦν αἰῶνα (2 Tim. iv, 10); there is
a wisdom which is "of this age"—σοφία τοῦ
αἰῶνος τούτου (1 Cor. ii, 6. Compare, also, 1 Cor.
i, 20; Luke xvi, 8 ; Eph. ii, 2).

(2) "By metonomy of the container for the contained, οἱ αἰῶνες denotes *the worlds, the universe*, that is, the aggregate of things contained in time," as opposed to κόσμος, or the world as contained in space. Thus we have: "Through whom also he made the worlds"—τοὺς αἰῶνας (Heb. i, 2); "By faith we understand that the worlds—τοὺς αἰῶνας—have been framed by the word of God" (Heb. xi, 3).

(3) Another signification of the term is duration without limitation, or *forever*. Thus in 2 Pet. iii, 18, we have: "To him be the glory both now and forever"—εἰς ἡμέραν αἰῶνος, literally, "unto the day which is eternity." In John vi, 51, we have: "If any man eat of this bread he shall live forever"—εἰς τὸν αἰῶνα, etc. Other forms of the word that express the same idea are εἰς πάντας τοὺς αἰῶνας—unto all the ages (Jude 25); εἰς τοὺς αἰῶνας τῶν αἰώνων—unto the ages of the ages (Rev. i, 6, etc.). When these phrases are used with a negative particle, as οὐ μή, or simply οὐ, they signify an unqualified

never, or *not forever*. Examples are as follows: "But whosoever drinketh of the water that I shall give him shall never thirst"—οὐ μὴ διψήσει εἰς τὸν αἰῶνα (John iv, 14); "Wherefore, if meat maketh my brother to stumble, I will eat no flesh for evermore"—οὐ μὴ φάγω κρέα εἰς τὸν αἰῶνα (1 Cor. viii, 13); "And the bond-servant abideth not in the house forever"—οὐ μένει ἐν τῇ οἰκίᾳ εἰς τὸν αἰῶνα (John viii, 35).

(4) In some cases the word signifies simply *a very long time*. "The same were the mighty men which were of old"—ἀπ' αἰῶνος (Gen. vi, 4. Compare, also, Luke i, 70; John ix, 32; Acts iii, 21; xv, 18).

From the substantive αἰών is derived the adjective αἰώνιος. That this word is used to signify "everlasting" would never have been questioned but for the possible implication of this fact in relation to the doctrine of future punishment. In the following instances it undoubtedly bears this meaning. "The eternal God" (Rom. xvi, 26); "For we know that if the earthly house of our tabernacle be dissolved, we have a building from God, a house not made with hands, eternal, in the heavens" (2 Cor. v, 1); "The eternal Spirit" (Heb. ix, 14); "And for this cause he is the mediator of a new covenant, that a death having taken place for the redemption of the transgressions that were under the first covenant, they that have been called may receive the promise of the eternal inheritance" (Heb. ix, 15); " Therefore I endure all things for the elect's sake, that they also may obtain the salvation which is in Christ Jesus with eternal glory" (2 Tim. ii, 10), etc.

It is also used, however, metaphorically or poetically (Hab. iii, 6) to signify indefinite or long time. But we would suggest that its metaphorical and poetic use is grounded upon, and derives its force from, its absolute signification. An illustration may be given in the use of our own word " eternal." Because this word signifies to us " everlasting " in an absolute sense, therefore its metaphorical use, as when we say "eternal hills" or "eternal laws," etc., has the force of meaning that such expressions convey to us.

The same remark may be made concerning the use of αἰώνιος in other than strictly metaphorical significations. Examples are as follows : " And I will give unto thee, and to thy seed after thee, the land of thy sojournings, all the land of Canaan, for an everlasting possession" (Gen. xvii, 8); "And this shall be an everlasting statute unto you" (Lev. xvi, 34). In these and other instances the absolute signification of the word furnishes ground for its secondary and limited use.

The Septuagint use of αἰών and αἰώνιος is of interest as illustrating the New Testament use, the latter in many respects being derived from the former. There they are used in translating עוֹלָם and עַד (with their plural forms, reduplications, and combinations), with which they have very similar meanings, though different etymological ideas. Some of the corresponding forms in Hebrew and Greek are as follows: עוֹלָם = αἰών; לְעוֹלָם = εἰς τὸν αἰῶνα; עוֹלָם עוֹלָמִים = αἰῶνες τῶν αἰώνων; עַד־עוֹלְמֵי עַד = ἕως τοῦ αἰῶνος ἔτι = "unto the time of eternity and on;" עוֹלָמִים = αἰώνιος. The following passages are examples in addition to those given above: "And the Lord said, My Spirit shall not strive with man forever" (Gen. vi, 3); "As I live forever" (Deut. xxxii, 40); "One generation goeth, and another generation cometh; and the earth abideth forever" (Eccl. i, 4); "But Israel shall be saved by the Lord with an everlasting salvation: ye shall not be ashamed nor confounded world without end" (Isa. xlv, 17).

When all the recognized and indisputable uses of αἰών and αἰώνιος in classic and in Old and New Testament writings are taken into the account, their influence in determining the question of the duration of future punishment is in themselves alone of little worth; but in connection with all the facts given on the subject, remembering their possible signification of "everlasting," they are of great importance.*

'Αίδιος. This word is found but twice in the New Testament, once in Rom. i, 20, "For the invisible things of him since the creation of the world are clearly seen, being perceived through the things that are made, even his everlasting [ἀίδιος] power and divinity," and once in Jude 6, "And angels which kept not their own principality, but left their proper habitation, he hath kept in everlasting [ἀιδίοις] bonds under darkness unto the judgment of the great day."

Much capital is made by some writers out of the fact that ἀίδιος, which, as they assert, is a much stronger word than αἰώνιος, is used but once in the New Testament in connection with the subject of future punishment. And then, they assert, where it is so used it cannot signify eternal punishment; for the "everlasting bonds" in which the fallen angels are kept "under darkness" last only "unto the judgment of the great day."

---

*We doubt if any orthodox writer claims more for these words, and yet many writers of the opposite class expend much time and labor in proving that the words do not always in the Scriptures signify " eternity."

Besides what has already been two or three times said as to the punishment of the lost after the judgment, we may ask if this word signifies so much more than αἰώνιος in the New Testament, as these writers assert. Paul, as we have seen, is the only writer besides Jude who uses the word. The signification of the word as used by him is not uncertain; but this same apostle who speaks of the "aidian" power and divinity of God speaks also in another place of the "æonian [αἰώνιος] God" (Rom. xvi, 26). Did he mean more when he used ἀίδιος in the one case than when he used αἰώνιος in the other? Can we translate "everlasting power and divinity" in the one case and "age-long God" in the other, and believe the apostle had any such distinction in his thought? Must we not regard his use of the words as not only synonomous, but identical? Besides, St. Jude, in the same passage in which he speaks of "aidian bonds," speaks also of "æonian fire" (πῦρ αἰώνιον). Did he mean more by the one word than by the other? or did he use them as interchangeable?

Whatever the passage in Jude may or may not signify as to the punishment of the lost, we are persuaded from the above considerations that the claim that ἀίδιος would have been a better word in general to express the orthodox doctrine of future punishment than αἰώνιος has no foundation in the facts in the case. Indeed, this is tacitly, though inconsistently, granted in the assertion above referred to, that ἀΐδιος in the passage in question does *not* mean "everlasting."

3. Our third class of words are those that pertain to the condition or state of the lost. These terms are those upon which the Annihilationist bases his claim. As to this doctrine we will have more to say further on. For the present we are to deal with the terms simply from the stand-point of the present chapter. They are in all general respects identical, and so may be briefly considered together.

The claim made for them is that they signify the total destruction, not the eternal punishment, of the lost. This assertion is based partly upon the use of the terms in the Greek writers. Thus White says, "No fact in literature is capable of clearer demonstration than that the majority of these nouns and verbs, denoting *destruction* of some sort, are used by Plato again and again in the *Phædon*, a dialogue on immortality, expressly for the purpose of conveying the idea of the literal destruction or *extinction of the soul*" (*Life in Christ*, p. 360). "They are precisely the terms generally chosen in the New Testament to denote the punishment of the wicked, with this difference, that Plato says the soul will *not* suffer θάνατος, ἀπώλεια, ὄλεθρος, φθορά ; that it is *not* destined to ἀπολέσθαι, καταφθείρεσθαι, διαφθείρεσθαι, ἀποθνήσκειν; while the New Testament writers declare that wicked men *shall* suffer what is denoted by these terms. In Plato's dialogue these words stand for *extinction of life*, for that idea only, and in the strongest possible contrast to the idea of perpetuation of being. Our argument is that in the New Testament they signify precisely the same doom—the final and absolute *extinction of life* in the case of the wicked " (*ibid.*, p. 361). It is this latter claim that we wish chiefly to examine.

A word may be said, however, as to the classic use of these terms. It is not denied that Plato used them in the sense which Mr. White claims for them. But it is denied that this is their common classic signification. Dean Plumptre shows that the earliest use of the earliest form of ἀπόλλυμι did not signify extinction of conscious being, and reminds us that the New Testament writers, in their use of the words in question, were not influenced by Plato, but by the older Greek writers through the Septuagint. He says of the word ἀπόλλυμι in these writers: "Of any approach of its use in regard to men, of the destruction of conscious existence, there is, so far as I know, not a single instance." The colloquial use of the word was the same (*Spirits in Prison*, pp. 323, 324, 327).

That these words in their biblical use do not signify the annihilation of the wicked (a doctrine contrary to the assumed immortality of the soul everywhere in the Scriptures), but the utter ruin and loss of the soul, the following facts will abundantly demonstrate:

(1) θάνατος (and it will not be assumed that the other words can assert more in the matter than this word, or that they can prove annihilation if it does not) is used concerning the soul in this life under sin, in which case it clearly cannot mean annihilation or extinction. Instances are as follows: "Verily, verily, I say unto you, He that heareth my word, and believeth him that sent me, hath eternal life, and cometh not into judgment, but hath passed out of death into life" (John v, 24). "We know that we have passed out of death into life, because we love the brethren" (1 John iii, 14). Instances in which the kindred word νεκρός is used are as follows: "And you did he quicken, when ye were dead through

your trespasses and sins" (Eph. ii, 1). "And you, being dead through your trespasses and the uncircumcision of your flesh, you, I say, did he quicken together with him, having forgiven us all our trespasses" (Col. ii, 13). One notable passage in which three kindred words are found (θάνατος being one of them) is Rom. vii, 9–11: "And I was alive apart from the law once: but when the commandment came, sin revived, and I died [ἀποθνήσκω]; and the commandment, which was unto life, this I found to be unto death [εἰς θάνατον]: for sin, finding occasion, through the commandment beguiled me, and through it slew me [ἀποκτείνω]."

The figurative use of θάνατος, and its class of words, in other connections need only be referred to. Compare Rom. vi, 2, 7, 8, 11, etc.

(2) Ἀπόλλυμι (and with this the other words go likewise) is also used of a soul in sin in life. Examples are as follows: "And he spake unto them this parable, saying, What man of you, having a hundred sheep, and having lost [ἀπολέσας] one of them, doth not leave the ninety and nine in the wilderness, and go after that which is lost [τὸ ἀπολωλός], until he find it? . . . I say unto you, that even so there shall be joy in heaven over one sinner that repenteth, more

than over ninety and nine righteous persons, which need no repentance " (Luke xv, 3–7). "Or what woman having ten pieces of silver, if she lose [ἀπολέσῃ] one piece, doth not light a lamp, and sweep the house, and seek diligently until she find it? . . . Even so, I say unto you, there is joy in the presence of the angels of God over one sinner that repenteth" (Luke xv, 8–10). " For the Son of man came to seek and to save that which was lost [τὸ ἀπολωλός] " (Luke xix, 10); " For this my son . . . was lost [ἀπολωλώς], and is found " (Luke xv, 24).

The Septuagint use of the terms θάνατος and ἀπόλλυμι is the same as that in the New Testament, from which the latter is derived. There they are used in translating the Hebrew מות and אבד. It will be necessary simply to quote a few passages in illustration. " I have gone astray like a lost sheep [ὡς πρόβατον ἀπολωλός] " (Psa. cxix, 176). " And he shall set up an ensign for the nations, and shall assemble the outcasts [τοὺς ἀπολομένους] of Israel, and gather together the dispersed of Judah from the four corners of the earth " (Isa. xi, 12). " I will seek that which was lost [τὸ ἀπολωλός] " (Ezek. xxxiv, 16). "As I live, saith the Lord God, I have no pleasure in the death [θάνατος] of the wicked " (Ezek. xxxiii, 11).

"O Jerusalem, Jerusalem, thou that killest the prophets, and stonest them which are sent unto thee, how often would I have gathered thy children together, even as a hen gathereth her chickens under her wings, and ye would not! Behold, your house is left unto you desolate."—Matt. xxiii, 37, 38.

"How shall I give thee up, Ephraim? how shall I deliver thee, Israel? how shall I make thee as Admah? how shall I set thee as Zeboim? mine heart is turned within me, my repentings are kindled together."—Hos. xi, 8.

"And ye will not come to me, that ye might have life."—John v, 40.

"But to Israel he saith, All day long I have stretched forth my hands unto a disobedient and gainsaying people."—Rom. x, 21.

"Behold, I stand at the door, and knock: if any man hear my voice, and open the door, I will come in to him, and will sup with him, and he with me."—Rev. iii, 20.

CHAPTER IV.

The Ground of Future Endless Retribution; or, For What the Wicked are Punished Eternally.

IN the foregoing chapters we have considered the scriptural grounds of the doctrine of future endless retribution and presented and answered the objections and arguments of the Universalist, supplementing these considerations with a chapter on the New Testament terminology on the subject. It is now time to consider the question involved in the title of the present chapter: *for what* will the wicked be punished eternally?

The importance of this phase of the subject will be manifest to every one; especially when it is remembered how many false views have prevailed at one time or another, and in one part of the Christian Church or another, and how much confusion prevails to-day in the minds of many writers and teachers on both sides of the question with regard to it. It will be our aim in the present chapter to gather together the facts and considerations involved in this inquiry, and to seek the true solution of the difficulty in the answer of the Scriptures. We propose to consider first the things for which men will *not* be punished forever, or false views upon the subject, and then, positively, that for which they will be thus punished, or the ground of eternal guilt.

THINGS FOR WHICH THE WICKED WILL NOT BE PUNISHED ETERNALLY.

In general terms it may be said that no man will be punished in the other life for that over which he had no control, or for things for which he was not responsible, in this life. We have no doctrine upon the subject which denies the position that ability and responsibility are commensurate; none which assigns man to perdition for any other cause than personal demerit. The following doctrines cannot, therefore, be true:

1. That which assigns men to hell for the sin of Adam. This doctrine has played an influential part in the theology of the Church from the days of Augustine to the present time, and still lingers in creeds that do not trace their paternity through any direct line to this ancient father. A few sample quotations embodying the venerable error will be in place. The first we take from the Augsburg Confession, the first and most generally received symbol of the Lutheran

Church. In Article II, on "Original Sin," it says:

"Also they ['the churches with common consent among us'] teach that, after Adam's fall, all men begotten after the common course of nature are born with sin; that is, without the fear of God, without trust in him, and with fleshly appetite; and that this disease, or original fault, is truly sin, condemning and bringing eternal death now also upon all that are not born again by baptism and the Holy Spirit" (Schaff's *Creeds of Christendom*, vol. iii, p. 8).

In the Thirty-Nine Articles of the Church of England, on the same subject, Article IX, is the following:

"Original sin standeth not in the following of Adam (as the Pelagians do vainly talk); but it is the fault and corruption of the nature of every man, that naturally is engendered of the offspring of Adam; whereby man is very far gone from original righteousness, and is of his own nature inclined to evil, so that the flesh lusteth always contrary to the spirit; and therefore in every person born into this world, it deserveth God's wrath and damnation* . . ." (*ibid.*, vol. iii, p. 493).

---

* It should be remembered that this last clause was left out of our "Articles of Religion" when abridged from the Thirty-Nine cf

Once more, in the Westminster Confession of Faith, Article VI, "Of the Fall of Man, of Sin, and of the Punishment Thereof," is the following:

" Every sin, both original and actual, being a transgression of the righteous law of God, and contrary thereunto, doth, in its own nature, bring guilt upon the sinner, whereby he is bound over to the wrath of God and curse of the law, and so made subject to death, with all miseries spiritual, temporal, and eternal" (*ibid.*, p. 616).

We repudiate this doctrine as irrational and unscriptural. We are concerned with it mostly, however, as unscriptural. This the following facts will demonstrate:

(1) The Scriptures every-where represent the guilt of man as *personal*, and not hereditary. Witness the following illustrative passages: "I the Lord search the heart, I try the reins, even to give every man according to his ways, according to the fruit of his doings" (Jer. xvii, 10); "The soul that sinneth, it shall die;" "The soul that sinneth, it shall die: the son shall not bear the iniquity of the father, neither shall the father bear the iniquity of the son; the right-

---

the Church of England by Mr. Wesley, and adopted by the Christmas Conference of 1784. As a Church we are, therefore, committed against the error.

eousness of the righteous shall be upon him, and the wickedness of the wicked shall be upon him" (Ezek. xviii, 4, 20); "And I say unto you, that every idle word that men shall speak, they shall give account thereof in the day of judgment" (Matt. xii, 36); "Who will render to every man according to his works" (Rom. ii, 6; compare Psa. lxii, 12; Prov. xxiv, 12; Jer. xxxii, 19; Matt. xvi, 27; 2 Cor. v, 10; Rev. ii, 23; xx, 12; xxii, 12); "So then each one of us shall give account of himself to God" (Rom. xiv, 12). And nowhere is it said in the Scriptures that a man shall give account to God for the sin of Adam, or of any one but himself.

Depravity is inherited, but not guilt; and it is with reference to this fact that all the passages that are frequently urged to prove inherited guilt, such as Eph. ii, 3, "And were by nature children of wrath," * and Rom. v, 12-21, find their proper interpretation.

---

* We include Eph. ii, 3, among this class of passages because it is one of the strongholds of the advocates of inherited guilt, and by opponents of this doctrine is said simply to teach genetic depravity ; but we question if it has any direct reference to "original sin" in any sense. In the light of the context (verses 1-10) the passage seems to teach simply that those to whom it refers were "according to condition" before they received the gospel subjects of the divine wrath. In Paul's thought the contrast in the passage is between the Ephesian Christians as

(2) In the New Testament representations of the judgment the lost are assigned to punishment solely for their own sins. Examine Matt. xxv, 41-46; 2 Pet. ii; Rev. xx, 12-15; xxii, 10-15. In all of these passages the punishment of the wicked is represented as awarded on the ground of personal guilt in actual sin. In the story of Dives and Lazarus, moreover, no intimation is given that the former was in punishment for the sins of any but himself.

2. Again, the wicked will not be punished forever on the ground of an arbitrary reprobation. This doctrine differs from the one preceding in that it is confined to the Calvinistic creeds and theologies. No Arminian advocates unconditional election and reprobation, while some do hold to the doctrine of hereditary guilt.

Appealing to the only rule of faith on this as on every other doctrine—the Scriptures—we reject this teaching also, for the following chief reasons:

(1) It contradicts the many passages which

---

saved, and as living, formerly, according to the "course of this world," as "the rest" of the Gentiles. They, then, were "by nature" (φύσει), or according to natural condition or state as living in sin, "children of wrath [worthy of the divine wrath; compare the phrase "son of Gehenna" in Matt. xxiii, 15] even as the rest."

declare the free and universal purpose and provision of God for the "sins of the whole world." Familiar examples are as follows: " Behold, the Lamb of God, which taketh away the sin of the world!" (John i, 29); " For God so loved the world, that he gave his only begotten Son, that whosoever believeth on him should not perish, but have eternal life" (*ibid.*, iii, 16); "God was in Christ reconciling the world unto himself" (2 Cor. v, 19); "And he is the propitiation for our sins; and not for ours only, but also for the whole world " (1 John ii, 2).

The Calvinist has one all-convenient recourse by which he can obviate the plain import of these gracious words of Scripture, namely, by dishonoring God in attributing to him an insincere purpose, according to the teaching which ascribes to him a "secret," as over against his "revealed," will, the one contradicting and belying the other; God, according to the latter, declaring to men his willingness and desire to save, and according to the former, withholding from the non-elect " effective " grace.

It is quite sufficient to reply to this, that if this assumption be true we are unable to know whether God's "revealed" will concerning the "elect" is a sincere will; and, for aught we can know to the contrary, all will be finally reprobate through the working out of his "secret" will. Thus the Calvinist by his own assumption takes the ground of confidence from beneath his own feet, and destroys all effective assurance of the salvation even of the saints. Thus, like the unlucky mechanic, he saws off the very limb on which he is sitting.*

(2) God explicitly says that he has no pleasure in the death of the wicked. In Ezekiel he asks and answers his own question pertaining to this

---

* Moderate New England Calvinism (the New Haven type) rejected this explanation of the difficulty on the ground of *two* wills, inconsistent and contradictory, and resorted to the view that God sincerely desires the salvation of all men, but that it is incompatible with the highest good of his system as a whole to efficiently cause the salvation of any but the elect. These latter are not loved more than others, but are chosen with reference to the general motive named, namely, the greatest possible good of the system as a whole. (Fisher, *Discussions in History and Theology*, pp. 325, 326.)

This doctrine implies that the best possible system God could arrange involved and necessitated the unconditional reprobation of some men, beyond their ability to choose or receive the contrary, to eternal death. It is held by Arminians (and was also held by the New Haven School of Calvinists) that the best possible system, under the divine wisdom and benevolence, involves freedom to sin with all its consequences, actual and possible; but this declares simply that the best order of things excludes a divine forceful prevention of sin, or the destruction of free moral agency. The distinctive doctrine of the New Haven theology holds that it is necessary for the best possible outcome in the created system that God should leave some men without

very subject. " Have I any pleasure in the death of the wicked? saith the Lord God: and not rather that he should return from his way, and live?" (chap. xviii, 23). The answer is in verse 32 of this same chapter, and in chapter xxxiii, 11 : "For I have no pleasure in the death of him that dieth, saith the Lord God : wherefore turn yourselves, and live ;" " Say unto them, As I live, saith the Lord God, I have no pleasure in the death of the wicked ; but that the

---

the efficient and necessary means of salvation, or, in other words, that the unconditional damnation of some men is a necessary means of the best possible system of things. The former doctrine makes the free agency of men the necessary element in such a system ; the latter makes divine unconditional election this necessary element.

But this doctrine, while better and profounder than the older and more common one discussed in the text, is also freighted with insuperable difficulties. It devolves upon advocates of the doctrine to prove that the so-called necessity is real. As an assumption it can only have weight upon the truthfulness of the prior assumption of an unconditional election and reprobation. In other words, it is of significance at all only on the assumption that the Calvinistic doctrine of election and its corollary are exegetically proven. But this we do not allow. Besides, the doctrine is, equally with the other, contrary to the assumed ability of all men to repent and be saved in the Scriptures, and with the universal provisions of grace with this end in view, also given in the Scriptures and admitted by the Calvinist.

No form of Calvinism will ever be able to reconcile its doctrines of partial election and grace with the freeness and provision of grace offered to all men upon assumed conditions of ability on the part of all to accept salvation.

wicked turn from his way and live: turn ye, turn ye from your evil ways; for why will ye die, O house of Israel." In the New Testament the divine revelation is equally explicit. "Who willeth that all men should be saved, and come to the knowledge of the truth" (1 Tim. ii, 4). "The Lord is not slack concerning his promise, as some count slackness; but is long-suffering to you-ward, not wishing that any should perish, but that all should come to repentance" (2 Pet. iii, 9).

In view of the positive divine declarations of these passages, how singular that the "good pleasure of his will" (Eph. i, 5) could ever have been made to involve, in some cases, the eternal and unconditional reprobation of men to death! Surely it is time for a revision of the Westminster Confession of Faith!

Our general Arminian position makes it unnecessary to notice the present false doctrine at any greater length.

3. Nor will human beings be assigned to hell for a failure to receive what was not within their power to receive; but which, through the neglect or providential inability of others, was not given to them. We refer in this place to the two false doctrines which have assigned persons

to perdition for not having received baptism over which they had no control, and for not having heard the Gospel. These theological errors likewise demand brief consideration.

Both of them have occupied a large place in the teaching of the creeds, and are entertained and taught in certain large sections of the Church to-day. "Zwingli was the first to emancipate the *salvation of children* dying in infancy from the supposed indispensable condition of water-baptism" (Schaff's *Creeds of Christendom*, vol. i, p. 378). "The Roman Catholic Church, in keeping with her doctrine of original sin and guilt, and the necessity of water-baptism for salvation (based upon Mark xvi, 16, and John iii, 5), teaches the salvation of all baptized, and the *condemnation* of all *unbaptized* children; assigning the latter to the *limbus infantum* on the border of hell, where they suffer the mildest kind of punishment, namely, the negative penalty of loss (*pœna damni*, or *carentia beatificæ visionis*), but not the positive pain of feeling (*pœna sensus*). St. Augustine first clearly introduced this wholesale exclusion of all unbaptized infants from heaven" (*ibid.*, p. 379). "The Lutheran creed retains substantially the Catholic view of baptismal regeneration, and hence limits infant salvation to those who enjoy this means of grace; allowing, however, some exceptions within the sphere of the Christian Church, and making the damnation of unbaptized infants as mild as the case will permit. At present, however, there is scarcely a Lutheran divine of weight who would be willing to confine salvation to *baptized* infants" (*ibid.*, pp. 379, 380). The creed of the Greek Church is in keeping with the Roman Catholic and the Lutheran.* As to the salvation of the heathen Dr. Schaff says : "Before Zwingli it was the universal opinion that there can be no salvation outside of the visible Church (*extra ecclesiam nulla salus*). Dante, the poet of the mediæval Catholicism, assigns even Homer, Aristotle, Virgil, to hell" (*ut supra*, p. 382). Zwingli was an exception in his own age. "Luther was horrified at the idea that even 'the godless Numa' (!) should be saved, and thought that it falsified the whole Gospel, without which there can be no salvation" (*ibid.*). This doctrine is taught to-day. In de-

---

* A strange coincidence in history is the fact that through the logical exigency of two false doctrines (predestinarianism and a false view of baptism as a necessary and saving ordinance) innocent children have been assigned to that hell whose earthly symbol (Gê Hinnom, the valley of Hinnom on the south and west of Jerusalem) was at one time the place of the worship of the god Molech, whose delight was in the cries of burning children.

fense of it Dr. Charles Hodge says: "We must not charge the ignorance and consequent perdition of the heathen upon God. The guilt rests on us. We have kept to ourselves the bread of life, and allowed the nations to perish" (*Systematic Theology*, vol. i, p. 31). Thus Dr. Hodge charges the damnation of the heathen upon the neglect of the Church.*

Both doctrines are alike contrary to the spirit and explicit teaching of the Scriptures. As to the first, it may be urged in general that *unbaptized* children were by Christ declared to be examples and subjects of his kingdom (Matt. xviii, 2-5; xix, 13-15; Mark ix, 36, 37; x, 13-16; Luke xviii, 15-17). As such they could not be lost. It would seem a more rational inference to say, Because they are Christ's they should be baptized, than to say that they should be baptized in order to be made Christ's.† As to the

---

* The history of this latter error is given at some length in Plumptre's *Spirits in Prison*, chap. vi.

† With reference to the passages that have been urged to prove the damnation of children unbaptized (Mark xvi, 16; John iii, 5), it may be said: (1) That both imply the responsibility of those of whom they speak. In the first instance Christ evidently meant that condemnation would rest upon those who *refused* the Gospel. In the second case no reference is made to children, and the inference of their damnation if unbaptized from the passage assumes that Christ must deal with children

second doctrine, it is only necessary to urge the words of the apostle Peter when sent to Cornelius, " Of a truth I perceive that God is no respecter of persons: but in every nation he that feareth him, and worketh righteousness, is acceptable to him" (Acts x, 34, 35); and to suggest, still further, that, according to Paul in Rom. i and ii, and elsewhere, even Peter's revelation was not the fullest light to come on the subject of the heathen in apostolic times. According to the former apostle the following points seem to embrace the doctrine of the Scriptures upon the subject: (1) That the Gentile is condemned by disobedience to the light of nature (this including both the teaching of nature and the universal presence of the Holy Spirit [Rom. i, 20; 2, 12, 14, 15]; compare John i, 9); (2) That God does not require of him to live above what is revealed to him, or above his opportunities (Acts xvii, 30); (3) That even by this standard, while con-

---

in an economy of grace as he does with adults, an assumption without foundation in fact, as the passages above given in the text demonstrate. Men are sinful and responsible, children are not; and it is folly in any case to draw a conclusion with reference to the innocent and irresponsible from words intended for the responsible and sinful. (2) It cannot be proved that John iii, 5, signifies more than the necessity of the new birth by the Holy Spirit *symbolized* (not *produced*) by baptism. It no doubt involves the duty of Christian baptism.

demned for failure, justification cannot come; for none can be justified by keeping the law, whether that law is given in nature or in the Scriptures (Rom. iii, 19-30) ; (4) That while God requires all men to strive to live up to the measure of light possessed, still occasional failure, or even continual conscious deficiency, while to be repented of, does not exclude from the possession and privileges of divine sonship. Willful and persistent rejection of the light possessed seems the only bar to the divine favor and acceptance.*

Other false doctrines on the subject of eternal guilt are (1) That which makes subscription to a creed essential to salvation, and (2) That which makes membership in a visible church necessary.

Illustrations of the first error are as follows: " Whosoever will be saved before all things, it is necessary that he hold the Catholic faith : which faith except every one do keep whole and undefiled, without doubt he shall perish everlastingly"

---

* In proof of this last point we refer the reader to those passages in Paul's epistles which seek to correct sins in many *believers*, as, for example, 1 Cor. vi, 15-20 ; Eph. iv, 17-32 ; Col. iii, 1-10. The reader is also referred for a fuller statement of this point to an article by the writer in the *Methodist Review* for January, 1889, pp. 79-85.

(*Symbolum Quicunque, or The Athanasian Creed.* See the whole creed in Schaff, *ut supra*, vol. ii, pp. 66-70); "I do, at this present, freely profess and truly hold this true Catholic faith, without which no one can be saved" (Profession of the Tridentine Faith, A. D., 1564. See Schaff, vol. i, pp. 96-98; vol. ii, pp. 207-210). The famous bull "Unam Sanctam" of Bonifice VIII. (1302) declared it necessary to salvation to believe the Roman pontiff supreme in all secular (governmental) affairs, as well as spiritual, and the Vatican Council of 1870 confirmed this doctrine in its decree concerning papal absolutism and infallibility, and set its condemning seal upon an opposing doctrine in the following language: "But if any one—which may God avert—presume to contradict this our definition: let him be anathema" (Schaff, vol. ii, p. 271).

As to the second false doctrine, the Cyprionic rule "*extra ecclesiam nulla salus*" has not only been applied to the heathen, but to nominal Christians, and even to genuine followers of Christ outside of some particular visible Communion. Thus " in the seventeenth century the Romanists excluded the Protestants, the Lutherans the Calvinists, the Calvinists the Arminians, from the kingdom of heaven" (Schaff, as above, vol. i, p. 384). The Romish doctrine is no better to-day.

With regard to these doctrines the following may be said: As to the first, (1) That while the New Testament makes unbelief in the Gospel a condemning sin (Mark xvi, 16*), there is no warrant for the extension of this principle to the creeds of men, except in so far as they embody and rightly interpret the Gospel; and (2) That then it is safer and less misleading to place the condemnation on the ground of the teaching of the New Testament than on the teaching of human creeds. Against the second doctrine, (1) That it contradicts the New Testament principles above announced concerning the heathen (this larger relation of the Gospel to those outside of the visible Church including the lesser one concerning the Christians in nominally Christian countries outside of any Church: much more those in the different denominations); (2) That it makes salvation depend upon an agency established to foster and develop the Christian life, not to create it. The Holy Spirit is the agent of eternal life (John iii, 3, 5, 7, 8); (3) That

---

* According to our revisers this text is in the midst of a doubtful passage (Mark xvi, 9-20): but the truth it involves is given elsewhere (John xii, 48).

there have been, and are to-day, devout Christians outside of the visible Church, as, for example, the Society of Friends.*

We teach it to be the duty of all to belong to the visible Church and receive its sacraments, because it is a divine institution (Matt. xvi, 18; 1 Tim. iii, 15) and means of grace, and because without membership in it it could not be sustained, and its work of saving the world and edifying believers properly done. We teach, also, that a positive refusal to unite with the Church, in the light of a clear conviction of this as a duty, will exclude from the kingdom of heaven. But this is placing the condemnation of such persons as thus refuse on the ground of positive sin, for "To him therefore that knoweth to do good, and doeth it not, to him it is sin" (Jas. iv, 17). All of this, however, is very different from making the salvation of men depend upon connection with a particular Church, or with any Church without qualification.

The Ground of Eternal Guilt.

Having considered these more prominent and historic errors, we now turn to the positive side of

---

* This society of Christians cannot be said to be a Church, because they ignore the sacraments.

our subject : for what will the wicked be punished eternally ? or what is the ground of eternal guilt ? In our treatment of this important topic two very distinct questions must be taken into the account : (1) That for which eternal death is merited, and (2) That for which this death will be inflicted under an economy of grace. This division of our subject will save us much confusion of thought, and help us the better to understand certain current errors relating to it.

1. That for which men deserve eternal death. In general terms it may be said that sin, or all responsible wrong-doing, merits eternal death. Or, to put the thought in other words, all transgression of the divine law, which is sin, deserves the affixed and necessary penalty of that law. In the light of this definition it will be found that all who have reached the age of responsible action have justly subjected themselves, through actual sin, to the wrath of God, and deserve his condemnation.*

This doctrine is the reiterated teaching of the Scriptures, and the background of the divine

---

* This is not the place to discuss the question of the relation of children to the atonement, and we need only say that, not being sinners in any true definition of sin, their relation to Christ must be wholly peculiar, as is their relation to probation and the new birth.

mercy and grace in the atonement. It is because we have sinned and come short of the glory of God, and deserve his just and necessary wrath and condemnation, that a merciful and gracious atonement was needed and possible. Otherwise Christ would not have died.

It is this fact, moreover, that shows the depth of the divine love for us in our redemption. It was to save us from a deserved perishing that God gave his only begotten Son.

These facts of Scripture are so well known, and so freely admitted, that a fuller statement of them is wholly needless; but, in a few words, their bearing upon the modern doctrine of a future probation must be considered.

This doctrine teaches that some men in this life, particularly the heathen, have not a sufficient probation. This means that they do not have a "fair chance" of eternal life here and now; and, if its logical implications are at all to be taken into the account, that all men do not deserve eternal death for the sins of this present time. In order to be worthy of death they must know and reject the revelation of God in the life and death of his Son—they must know and reject the historic Christ. Some carry their principle so far as to say that many in even nominally

Christian lands have not had sufficient opportunity of life to merit eternal punishment.

Our objections to this doctrine are involved in our statement above of the ground of future eternal guilt, and may be explicitly given as follows: (1) The doctrine is contrary to the fact that all men deserve death, whether they be Christian or heathen. "For we before laid to the charge both of Jews and Greeks, that they are all under sin" (Rom. iii, 9). "For all have sinned, and fall short of the glory of God" (Rom. iii, 23). On this fact of universal sinfulness and condemnation is built by Paul the fact of universal grace and atonement. If already sinful and condemned, men need no future probation through which to merit eternal death. They now deserve it. (2) The doctrine further contradicts the Scriptures by making the knowledge of Christ necessary for condemnation, whereas Christ came not to condemn the world, but to save it (John iii, 17). He found the world already guilty and condemned, and came to save it from its sin.

If the doctrine of a future probation is to be maintained, therefore, it must find ground elsewhere than in the demands of the divine justice. According to this, as said, all deserve death. If the doctrine is to be maintained, it must find support in a revelation of mercy according to divine grace. Our present continued probation is such; and if there is a future probation it must be one of grace also. This is the position that some advocates of the doctrine seem chiefly to occupy.

That a gracious second* probation is not explicity revealed in the Scriptures the advocates of the doctrine freely admit. They claim for it simply the ground of a legitimate inference from certain Scripture facts and teachings. These facts and inferences may be briefly considered, and then followed by a presentation of positive facts against the doctrine.

(1) Argument from the "absoluteness" or universality of the Christian religion. It is claimed that unless Christ be made known to all men somewhere before probation closes, the universality of his atoning sacrifice is limited;

---

* Advocates of this doctrine dislike to be charged with teaching a "second" probation, and assert that they advocate only a *sufficient* probation; if not here, then hereafter. That they are justly charged with teaching a "second" probation is manifest from the fact above shown (*from the fact of the condemnation of all*), that all have a sufficient probation here. Universal condemnation involves universal probation, sufficient and full. If men are to have a *future* probation, therefore, it will be a "second" probation. The one terms involves the other.

and as the heathen die without having known Christ, it is inferred that without a future probation they do not share the universal grace of the incarnation. This is the substance of a doctrine upon which volumes have been written.

Our response to this teaching is: 1.) That the assumption is true only on the ground of a moral influence doctrine of the atonement. We readily grant that if the influence of Christ's life and teaching is essential to salvation, then a knowledge of the historic Christ must be given to all men in probation, otherwise the atonement is not universal in its provision for the world's sin. But we do not admit the moral influence of the atonement as in any sense a cardinal or essential fact. We do not deny the fact of a moral influence in the atonement, but simply that it is an essential part thereof, or that it is a constituent element of atonement at all. 2.) That it contradicts the fact that some have been saved without the knowledge of Christ. No satisfactory account of the salvation of the Old Testament saints has ever been given consistently with the assumption that a knowledge of the historic Christ is essential to a proper probation. Abraham's faith, which was counted to him for righteousness (Rom. iv, 3; Gen. xv, 6).

was not a faith in the historic Christ, nor directly in Christ at all. So, also, of the other Old Testament characters.*

The absoluteness or universality of Christianity consists in the universal provision in the atonement for the forgiveness of the sins of the whole world, with the final complete regeneration and sanctification of all who through faith (in Christ for those who know him, and for those who do

---

* It is now admitted that *salvation* is possible without a knowledge of Christ, but not final *condemnation*. "It has not been our desire to show that no one could be saved, in the popular acceptation of the term, without the knowledge of God's redemptive love in Christ, but rather that those who apparently would not otherwise be saved, among whom we placed not the few but the many, might have the advantage of this knowledge before passing under judgment" (*Andover Review* for April, 1890, p. 441). This is extremely inconsistent. To say that a knowledge of Christ is essential to a proper probation, and then to admit that some can be saved without this knowledge, is to assert that the final destiny of some can be decided without an adequate probation—a contradiction of the fundamental thesis of these writers ; for they declare the necessity of a full and proper probation for even children and imbeciles. They first declare that a knowledge of Christ in probation is necessary for every one, and, after building upon this assumption the doctrine of a future probation for the heathen and certain other classes, they then, having gained all they desire from their doctrine thus established, through the exigency of certain clear cases of exception, overthrow that which they before established. They thus land in a denial of their own peculiar assumption, and help to re-establish and confirm the orthodox position that a knowledge of Christ is no essential element of a full and proper probation.

not, according to their opportunity and knowledge) seek to obey the dictates of the universal Spirit and the revelation given to them, whether in the Scriptures or in nature.*

(2) A gracious future probation is also argued on the ground of Christ's universal judgeship. Because Christ is to judge all men it is asserted that all men must know him; that Christ will not pronounce the doom of any soul who has not first known and rejected him. Thus the Andover reviewers say:

"It is clear that Christ is to be the judge. Christ is to be on the judgment-seat. . . . Now this means more than that in addition to his offices of Redeemer and Master Christ is also appointed Judge. It means that all men are to be judged under the Gospel; to be judged by their relation to Christ. . . . They are to come before his judgment-seat, not as those who are dragged there forcibly to meet a judge of whose person, character, and even existence they know nothing, but as those who are brought there as the necessary result of the knowledge of God which has been given them through him before

---

* For a fuller statement of this doctrine the reader is asked to consult the article before referred to in the *Methodist Review* of January, 1889.

whom they stand to be judged. When we read that Christ is to be the judge, we are to understand that the judgment will be a Christian judgment. . ." (*Progressive Orthodoxy*, p. 72).

In reply we would say: 1.) We most gladly recognize the gracious truth declared and illustrated in the fact that our *Judge* is our *Redeemer*. The most fundamental and characteristic fact in our redemption is exhibited in this twofold relationship of Christ to us. We are not to be judged by God out of Christ, or according to justice aside from mercy, but by God *in* Christ, or by justice according to a gracious redemption. By the first we are all condemned; by the second we may all be saved. But 2.) We see nothing in the mere fact of Christ's judgeship of all men to warrant the inference drawn from it aside from the explicit teaching of the Scriptures. Christ will judge all men in mercy and according to the provisions of his atoning sacrifice; but to say that he will not judge any but those who have known him is an assumption for which the Scriptures furnish no word of authority. 3.) The facts of the Scriptures are against it. We make the assertion here, and postpone its proof to another place, further on.

(3) Argument from the incarnation. It is

argued that Christ, in taking upon him our nature and becoming God-man, practically demonstrated the need of a knowledge of himself for the salvation of men; and that for the fulfillment of the purpose of the incarnation all men must in probation be brought into a relation of knowledge to God thus manifested in the flesh. This argument is the burden of the second chapter in *Progressive Orthodoxy*, although there not very explicity stated as such. It is one phase of the general argument from the absoluteness or universality of the Christian religion (see chap. ix, p. 256), but looked at from its own special stand-point.

In this statement of the argument we have placed upon it the best construction that we believe to be possible. Our objections are: 1.) While the incarnation was an essential element of the work of Christ in redemption (Phil. ii, 6-8; Heb. ii, 16-18; iv, 15, 16), and fulfills an important place in the evangelization of the world, that a knowledge of it is essential to salvation is what remains to be proved. The proof has not yet been given. But, on the other hand, 2.) The fact above urged in another connection, but which equally applies here, that some have been saved without this relationship of knowledge to the incarnate Christ, is positive proof against it.

(4) Another argument is based upon the assumption that the Holy Spirit can find sufficient material alone in the life, death, and teaching of our Lord for his efficacious and proper work in saving the lost. It is said in proof that the heathen—the great mass of them—are very corrupt, and in this condition cannot be saved. The alternate, these writers assert, is either that Christ must be made known to the heathen somewhere in probation, or the vast majority of them be forever lost.

In objection, besides urging the ever-recurring "exceptional cases" of regeneration without the knowledge of Christ, especially in the Old Testament, with which the Andover professors find much difficulty at every point, we may say that their cardinal mistake lies in the assumption that regeneration and morality must always coincide, or that they are inseparable in their lower, as well as higher, stages of development. That they are not may be proved, not only from the imperfect cases of morality in the Old Testament (for example, the cases of Abraham and Jacob), but from the same imperfection in many Christians of New Testament times, and even in ourselves. A thorough study of the subject will reveal that, while regeneration depends upon the inner working of the Holy Spirit, morality depends largely upon knowledge ; and that morality may exist without corresponding regeneration, and regeneration also in many cases without its corresponding and proper morality. Our inference from these facts is that many of the devout, though superstitious and even immoral, heathen may be, and most likely are, regenerate, and only need more perfect knowledge for their moral development and sanctification. For a further statement of this point we must refer the reader once more to our article in the *Methodist Review* for January, 1889.

(5) It is argued, further, that the condemning sin under the Gospel is unbelief, and that the heathen cannot be guilty of this sin without a knowledge of Christ. The inference is easy.

To this it may be said: 1.) That faith in Christ is the only way of salvation according to the Scriptures (Rom. iii, 22, 25, 26, 30; v, 1; xi, 20, etc.), and yet Cornelius was accepted of God before he had heard of Christ (Acts x, 34, 35). 2.) The passages that speak of unbelief in Christ as the condemning sin evidently refer to cases where Christ is *known*. The *preaching* of the

Gospel precedes the condemning unbelief of the Gospel (Mark xvi, 15, 16).

(6) A future probation is also inferred from so incidental a fact as the raising to life of the dead (Mark v, 42; Luke vii, 11-17; John xi), and from Paul's supposed prayer for Onesiphorus, after the latter's decease (2 Tim. i, 16-18; iv, 19).

As to the first case, Dorner says: "A proof that, according to the New Testament, the time of grace does not expire with death by a universal law, is found in Christ's raisings of the dead; for example, the youth at Nain received through resurrection from the dead a prolongation of the time of grace, through which Christ's love first became known to him" (*System of Christian Doctrine*, vol. iv, p. 409).

It may be said, however, that there is no reason for supposing that this young man was not saved at death (Lazarus and the daughter of Jairus certainly were), and if so his return to earth would not make any change in the outcome of his life. His probation, therefore, was practically and really closed at his first decease. Besides, the Andover Future Probationists confess that the argument based upon these facts is extremely uncertain. They say: "Inferences from the resurrection of Lazarus and of the widow's son, and from their subsequent opportunities, have always appeared to us very shadowy" (*Progressive Orthodoxy*, p. 101).

As to the case of Onesiphorus, 1.) it is not beyond doubt that he was dead; 2.) the so-called prayer of Paul in his behalf seems no more than an expression of good-will toward him. It certainly was not a formal and direct prayer. But 3.) if we must suppose he was dead, and if we regard Paul's parenthetical expression, "The Lord grant unto him to find mercy of the Lord in that day," a true prayer, such as would authorize us also to pray for the dead, it must be remembered that Onesiphorus was a Christian, and that no further inference could be drawn from the fact than that prayers might be offered for the *righteous* dead. This is the doctrine of the Church of Rome.

(7) Other passages which are said to furnish ground for this doctrine are as follows : " Then began he to upbraid the cities wherein most of his mighty works were done, because they repented not. Woe unto thee, Chorazin ! woe unto thee, Bethsaida! for if the mighty works had been done in Tyre and Sidon which were done in you, they would have repented long ago

in sackcloth and ashes. Howbeit I say unto you, it shall be more tolerable for Tyre and Sidon in the day of judgment, than for you. And thou, Capernaum, shalt thou be exalted unto heaven? thou shalt go down unto Hades: for if the mighty works had been done in Sodom which were done in thee, it would have remained until this day. Howbeit I say unto you, that it shall be more tolerable for the land of Sodom in the day of judgment, than for thee" (Matt. xi, 20-24); "And whosoever shall speak a word against the Son of man, it shall be forgiven him; but whosoever shall speak against the Holy Spirit, it shall not be forgiven him, neither in this world, nor in that which is to come" (Matt. xii, 32); "Because Christ also suffered for sins once, the righteous for the unrighteous, that he might bring us to God; being put to death in the flesh, but quickened in the spirit; in which also he went and preached unto the spirits in prison, which aforetime were disobedient, when the long-suffering of God waited in the days of Noah, while the ark was a preparing, wherein few, that is, eight souls, were saved through water" (1 Pet. iii, 18-20); "For unto this end was the gospel preached even to the dead, that they might be judged according to men in the flesh, but live according to God in the spirit " (1 Pet. iv, 6*).†

As to the first passage, it is said that if the ancient cities there referred to, " had they seen what the Jews saw, would have repented in sackcloth and ashes, they would have been saved, which therefore implies that if the time of grace expired for them with death they would be damned for not seeing and knowing Christ, which was not their fault " (Dorner, *System of Christian Doctrine*, vol. iv, p. 410). As to the second passage, it is said: " When, further, Christ says of a sin, that it is forgiven neither in this nor in the next life, whereas other sins are forgiven in this world without limitation, this contains a testimony that other sins, save the sin against the Holy Ghost, may be forgiven in the next world " (*ibid.*). The two passages in First Peter are the strongholds of this doctrine, and

---

*Compare Acts ii, 27, 31. Dorner thinks that Eph. iv, 8-10, has no reference to Christ's Hadean descent (*System of Christian Doctrine*, vol. iv, p. 128).

† We omit reference here to such passages as 1 Tim. ii, 4-6 ; Luke xix, 10 ; 1 John ii, 2, given by Dorner in favor of this doctrine, for the manifest reason that " to quote such passages to prove the broader view seems like trifling with the divine testimony." They are not used by the Andover professors. Besides, we have already sufficiently considered them in connection with the doctrine of Universalism in the second chapter.

it is claimed that in them is furnished a comparatively direct testimony concerning it.

Without attempting to enter into a full discussion of these much disputed passages of Scripture, it will be sufficient to say that one all conclusive fact against the doctrine of a future probation being inferred from them is that whatever the passages may signify as to a possible hope for some after this life, they cannot signify a future *probation;* for the representation in each case is entirely on the ground of things done in this life. It will be more tolerable for Tyre and Sidon and Sodom in the judgment than for Chorazin, Bethsaida, and Capernaum; but in all cases reference is undoubtedly intended to the earthly sins of these cities. So, also, if we are to suppose that Matt. xii, 32, signifies a possible forgiveness in the other life for all sins but the sin against the Holy Ghost, still it is the forgiveness of sins committed in this life. No intimation is given of the forgiveness of sins committed after death.* Likewise, in the case of the ante-

---

* It is doubtful, however, whether this passage, as suggested in another place, signifies more than what has been called an "emphasized negative." Dr. Love also suggests the following: "Some Jews, perhaps not many, previous to and at the time of Christ, believed that some of their people, suddenly cut off by death, though righteous, did not have passed upon them the full

diluvians, reference is made only to their earthly "disobedience" (1 Pet. iii, 20).

Future Probationists unwittingly overlook the fact that their doctrine involves the idea that *in the other life* sins may be both committed and forgiven. This is implicit in the very idea of future probation. Before the passages above given, therefore, can be urged as favoring this doctrine, they must be shown to have reference to sins committed in that life, and not merely to the possible forgiveness *there* of sins committed *here*. That they have no such reference we have seen.

In concluding this brief survey of the doctrine of a future probation, we would urge against it, positively, that not only do the Scriptures represent the outcome in the other life as wholly

---

act of forgiveness until they reached the other world. Some of them believed in *prayer* for such departed ones, as will hereafter be shown. On similar grounds, baptism for the dead was practiced by a few among the early nominal Christians, though generally discountenanced. A *living* Christian was baptized for an unbaptized *dead* Christian (1 Cor. xv, 29). By a few it was thought that without receiving such baptism the departed unbaptized could not be received into bliss. Knowing this belief among some of his hearers concerning the forgiveness of the dead who had suddenly been cut off, Jesus, without at all lending his sanction to that view, may have added the phrase, 'nor in that which is to come,' thus cutting off a groundless hope" (*Future Probation Examined*, p. 259).

dependent upon this life, without any intimation that acts there will be taken into the account in deciding moral and spiritual destiny (Matt. x, 32, 33; Rom. ii, 6-10; 2 Cor. v, 10; Gal. vi, 7, 8; Col. iii, 24, 25; Rev. xxii, 12, etc.), but in the representations of the judgment all punishment is for sins in this life (Matt. xxv, 41-46; Rev. xx, 12-15).

It must be remembered that the doctrine of a future probation necessarily assumes that some sins for which punishment will be awarded in the judgment will have been committed in the intermediate state, unless it be affirmed that all will in that state decide for Christ; and even then it would have to be said that the rewards of the righteous are also, according to these representations, for deeds in this life (Matt. xxv, 34-40, etc.). Now, with punishment and reward in the judgment solely for acts of this life, according to New Testament representations of the judgment, how maintain an after-death probation in which men may so act as to be saved or finally lost for the deeds of that state? On the ground of these facts the doctrine of an after-death probation will have to be surrendered, whatever other gracious truth the passages, or some of them, urged in its favor may teach us. (See chapter v.)

2. That for which eternal death will be inflicted under the Gospel. We now come to that part of our present topic which most concerns us. We have seen that for which men will not be punished forever, and that for which eternal death is merited according to the Scriptures, and we now inquire as to that for which this deserved death will be inflicted under the Gospel, or under an economy of mercy and grace.

Our answer to this inquiry is implicit in what has already been said. We have seen that all deserve death for responsible sin, or for a willful violation of the divine commandments, and have intimated that this was the reason and ground of the divine mercy and forgiveness in Christ. We are now prepared to appreciate the teaching of the Scriptures when they assert that there is no other way of salvation than that offered in Christ. " And in none other is their salvation : for neither is there any other name under heaven, that is given among men, wherein we must be saved " (Acts iv, 12). From all this the inference is easy that eternal death will be inflicted only in the case of him who rejects the divine way of forgiveness. For him who " hath trodden under foot the Son of God, and hath counted the blood of the covenant . . . an unholy thing, and hath done despite unto the Spirit of grace " "there remaineth no more a sacrifice for sins, but a certain fearful expectation of judgment, and a fierceness of fire which shall devour the adversaries" (Heb. x, 26-31). There is no atonement for the rejection of Christ, and it is this act, therefore, that leaves the soul exposed to all the deserved wrath of a violated divine law, and which is consequently, under the Gospel, that which damns forever. We deserved death before Christ came. From this he came to deliver us. If we refuse the deliverance offered in him, we remain lost beyond the power of divine grace to save. Our hell is made by rejecting the only way of life, and is made forever.

That this is the teaching of the Scriptures none who have accepted our doctrine thus far will be disposed to question. Other illustrative passages in addition to those given above are as follows: " And she shall bring forth a son; and thou shalt call his name Jesus; for it is he that shall save his people from their sins" (Matt. i, 21); " To him bear all the prophets witness, that through his name every one that believeth on him shall receive remission of sins" (Acts x, 43); " For all have sinned, and fall short of the glory of God; being justified freely by his grace through the redemption that is in Christ Jesus: whom God set forth to be a propitiation, through faith, by his blood, to show his righteousness, because of the passing over of the sins done aforetime, in the forbearance of God; for the showing, I say, of his righteousness at this present season: that he might himself be just, and the justifier of him that hath faith in Jesus " (Rom. iii, 23-26); " But God commendeth his love toward us, in that, while we were yet sinners, Christ died for us. Much more then, being now justified by his blood, shall we be saved from the wrath of God through him " (Rom. v, 8, 9); " He that believeth and is baptized shall be saved; but he that disbelieveth shall be condemned" (Mark xvi, 16); " I am come a light into the world, that whosoever believeth on me may not abide in the darkness. . . . He that rejecteth me, and receiveth not my sayings, hath one that judgeth him : the word that I spake, the same shall judge him in the last day " (John xii, 46, 48); " Verily, verily, I say unto you, He that believeth hath eternal life " (John vi, 47); " He that eateth my flesh and drinketh my blood hath eternal life " (John vi, 54), etc.*

---

* It will be noted that "rejecting" Christ (John xii, 48) is the same as unbelief (*ibid.*, verse 46). We reject Christ through

While both by the logic of our general premises concerning sin and redemption, and by the plain and specific teaching of the sacred Scriptures, we are led to this conclusion—that the rejection of Christ is the only damning sin under the Gospel—we are yet called upon to notice, according to the same Scriptures, the different possible forms of this all important sin.

(1) The direct sin of rejecting Christ. This is possible only where Christ is known, and it assumes the form of actual or practical unbelief. The Scriptures always assume that this unbelief is occasioned by a willful rejection of the light given. "If any man willeth to do his will, he shall know of the teaching, whether it be of God, or whether I speak from myself" (John vii, 17). "I said therefore unto you, that ye shall die in your sins: for except ye believe that I am he, ye shall die in your sins" (John viii, 24). "He that believeth on him is not judged: he that believeth not hath been judged already, because he hath not believed on the name of the only

---

unbelief. Also, "receiving" Christ and "believing on him" and "eating and drinking his flesh and blood" are but different New Testament ways of saying the same thing. We do not eat Christ in the eucharist, as the Romanists say, but by faith we receive him spiritually. The forty-seventh and fifty-fourth verses of John vi express the same truth.

begotten Son of God. And this is the judgment, that light is come into the world, and men loved the darkness rather than the light; for their works were evil " (John iii, 18, 19). The belief in Christ that saves, on the other hand, involves a belief in him as divine (1 John v, 9, 10, *et passim*). Unitarianism has a fearful sin to answer for according to the New Testament.

This rejection of Christ through unbelief that damns may be either his rejection as he is presented to men (Mark xvi, 16), or a final falling away from a faith that once saved (Heb. vi, 4-8; x, 26-31*). In both cases the sin may, in the outcome, amount to the sin against the Holy Ghost.

(2) The sin against the Holy Ghost. This sin is presented in the New Testament as a separate sin from the mere matter of unbelief (Matt. xii,

---

*These passages of Scripture must not be thought, however, to teach that the simple act of falling away from Christ is unpardonable, or that once to have known Christ and to have rejected him admits of no return, but must be read in the light of the circumstances of the case. The writer is speaking to the Jews who had accepted Christ and who were in danger of apostasy. He easily foresaw that if they should give up their faith in our Lord it would be impossible to renew *them* unto repentance. The circumstances of the case would make their sin peculiarly grievous, and would involve a total denial of Jesus as Lord (a thing that is not done in every case of backsliding), and would consequently foreclose all return to salvation and life.

22-32; Mark iii, 22-30; Luke xii, 10; 1 John v, 16), and as such demands separate consideration.

According to the account in Matthew and Mark, Christ had just healed a man that was possessed with a devil, and had restored his sight and speech. The people were amazed at this wonderful demonstration of supernatural power, and exclaimed in acknowledging faith: "Is not this the son of David?"—the expected Messiah. But when the Jewish leaders—the Pharisees and scribes—heard of the event, and how the people were being led by it to acknowledge Jesus as the Christ, in order to rebut this divine testimony to Jesus and call the people back from their acknowledgment of him, they declared that Jesus in casting out devils—a fact they did not deny—did so by the power of Satan. It was equivalent to saying that Christ was in league with Satan, and was in reality attributing to the devil the work of the Holy Ghost. The sin must have been a deliberate one on the part of these Jewish leaders, and must have been committed in the clear conviction that their attribution of the work of the Spirit to the evil one was a lie against the Holy Ghost. Their motive was to retain the confidence of the people in themselves and to withhold them from reposing it in Christ:

or, rather, they would dissuade the people from believing in Christ in order that they might retain their thievish and selfish hold upon them (John x, 8, 10, 12, 13). This deliberate sin Jesus said was blasphemy against the Holy Ghost, and that for it there was no forgiveness. So willful a rejection of the light given them closed the door of pardon upon these men.*

There is a strong theological tendency which seeks to resolve the damning sin of the New Testament into this sin against the Holy Ghost. There can be no doubt, as above said, that the final outcome of rejecting Christ amounts to this sin, but we think it truer to the New Testament teaching to represent the sin that damns as definitive unbelief, and to represent the sin against the Holy Ghost, as the Scriptures do, as one form or manifestation, perhaps the culminating form, of this sin. Certain it is, as above seen, that the sin that damns is unbelief, or the final rejection of Christ.

---

* We do not see how this conclusion can be avoided when it is remembered that Mark says that Jesus spoke of this sin "*because*" the Jews said, "He hath an unclean spirit" (iii, 30). Besides, the impression we get from the whole narrative is not that Jesus was warning these men of a sin they were in danger of committing (Dorner and others), but that he was speaking of a sin they had already committed.

But however we may regard these two sins as related to each other, there can be no doubt that either, or both, presupposes a persistent course in sinful development. No man by a misstep can fall into the guilt that damns forever under the Gospel. It must in every case be a deliberate act, or, better still, the culmination of many such acts. In this we entirely coincide with Müller when he says: "Unthinking recklessness, as such, is perfectly secure from the sin against the Holy Ghost" (*Christian Doctrine of Sin*, vol. ii, p. 421), and as well, we may add, against definitive unbelief; positing, however, that this sin persisted in, as well as every other sin, will no doubt ultimately lead to the sin of final unbelief; for sin, however much it is begun and continued in unthinking recklessness, or in any other spirit, becomes more and more, as time goes on and it continues, a matter of deliberate choice, with its corresponding rejection of the good. Sin is unsafe in any case; purposely chosen and persisted in until the close of life, it becomes final in the rejection of Christ, and forever damns. The best and only safe time to cease sinning and turn to the Lord is *now*.

(3) The sin for which condemnation is pronounced in the judgment according to Matt. xxv, 41-46. The sin for which final condemnation is

pronounced according to the representation in this passage is *unmercifulness*, as that for which the reward of the righteous is pronounced in the preceding verses is *mercifulness*, or acts of benevolence. " Depart from me, ye cursed, into the eternal fire which is prepared for the devil and his angels: for I was an hungered, and ye gave me no meat : I was thirsty, and ye gave me no drink : I was a stranger, and ye took me not in ; naked, and ye clothed me not ; sick, and in prison, and ye visited me not."

At first sight this seems wholly peculiar, and not what might have been expected from what has been above said. On the other hand, however, examination will reveal, not only that it is in perfect keeping with what has been said, but that it is a demonstration and illustration of it. The faith that saves is not a *fruitless* faith (Jas. ii, 14–26) ; nor is the unbelief that damns. Both have their corresponding fruits, and it is these fruits, or some of them, that are represented by our Lord as that for which condemnation or approval is respectively pronounced in the last day.* This is in

---

* It is worthy of note that one of the fruits of a "dead" faith, which is the same as unbelief, is, according to James, the very sin for which condemnation is pronounced in the judgment as given in Matthew. "But ye have dishonored the poor man " (chap. ii, 6. See the whole chapter).

keeping, moreover, with the representations of the judgment in other places, as, for example, in the parables of the Ten Virgins and the Talents in the foregoing part of this same chapter, and in the representations of the judgment in the Book of Revelation. In this latter place it is said that "the fearful, and unbelieving, and abominable, and murderers, and fornicators, and sorcerers, and idolaters, and all liars, their part shall be in the lake that burneth with fire and brimstone; which is the second death" (chap. xxi, 8). These, also, are some of the fruits of unbelief, and as such damn forever. Christ came to deliver us both from condemnation already merited, and also from the *power* of sin (Rom. vi, 1–8, etc.). Faith is the condition of deliverance from both. Unbelief leaves the soul subject to original condemnation, and a prey to the forces and powers of evil, and in the outcome is death. Consequently, by metonomy of the effect for the cause, the fruits of final unbelief are represented as furnishing the ground of final condemnation. We are damned for unbelief, but for unbelief that perpetuates and begets the sins that damn.

With this understanding of the passage in question, it is immaterial to us in this discussion whether it is taken to represent the general judgment of Christians and heathen alike, or simply that of the latter class of persons (Stier and others). The heathen and the nominally Christian are both alike justified by faith (Rom. iii, 30), and both alike, according to a necessary inference, condemned by unbelief; but both according to their opportunities and knowledge: the nominal Christian for faith or unbelief in Christ; the heathen for the same according to the light of nature and the manifestation of the Holy Spirit to him. In both cases, likewise, will there be the corresponding fruits of faith or unbelief, with their consequent approval or condemnation; but in this also for the heathen according to his light and opportunities (Luke xii, 48).

Implicit in these last statements is the much debated ground of final condemnation for those who in probation do not know the historic Christ. As some are received who do not believe in the historic Christ, so some will no doubt be condemned who do not have the opportunity of rejecting the historic Christ, but who in *reality* reject Christ; we do not object to the phrase " essential Christ," for we think it a convenient phrase to express the truth in the matter. If from deliberate and persistent choice the heathen reject the light they have, it is to be inferred that they would also reject greater light if given to them. If they will not hear the voice of God in the teaching of nature and by the Holy Spirit, neither would they believe though Christ were preached to them. (See Luke xvi, 31.) For " he that is faithful in a very little "—by application, the heathen who strives to live up to the measure of light possessed—" is faithful also in much." Such a heathen would be faithful also in the higher opportunities of the Gospel. "And he that is unrighteous in a very little "—by application, the dim light and opportunities of those who know not Christ—" is unrighteous also in much:" by equal application, such a person would be unrighteous also in the fuller light of the revelation of God in his Son (Luke xvi, 10).

This we think is the only consistent and scriptural teaching upon the subject. The heathen need no future probation in order to have a fair chance of eternal life in Christ; and it is equally certain that they will not be damned forever for not having known the historic Christ. The cause of missions must find some other ground of its inspiration than in the unqualified damnation of the heathen for not having been permitted to hear the Gospel—a thing for which they can in no wise be responsible, and which contradicts the universal grace and free opportunity of redemption for every man for eternal life.

To recapitulate, the conclusions of this chapter are: (1) That men in general will not be damned forever for that over which they have had no control, or for things for which they are not responsible. Ability and responsibility are equal. They will not, therefore, be condemned for the sin of Adam, nor for any arbitrary divine reprobation "for the glory of sovereign justice," nor for not having received baptism or heard the Gospel. Besides these matters for which persons are not responsible, and for which many have been assigned to an endless hell by an irrational and unscriptural theology, to be named as not necessary conditions of salvation are, subscription to a human creed, and membership in a, or the, visible Christian Church. (2) On the other hand, that for which all men deserve eternal death is responsible sin. By this standard all are guilty and deserve death; for "all have sinned and fall short of the glory of God." On the ground of this universal condemnation the doctrine of a future probation is seen to have no claim upon divine justice, and this fact lays upon the doctrine the demand of proving that it is graciously revealed and promised—a thing which it fails to do, and which is rebutted by positive Scripture facts against it. But from this universal condemnation Christ came to deliver us. Consequently, (3) That for which men are damned under the Gospel is definitive unbelief, or a final rejection of the only way of escape from their deserved condemnation. This sin of definitive unbelief has different forms and manifestations. Its common representation in the Scriptures is simple and final unbelief; but, as such, it no doubt amounts to the sin against the Holy Ghost. Among certain Pharisees and scribes in Christ's day it assumed the distinctive form of the special sin against the Holy Ghost; and while, as above said, all sin may be ultimately resolved into this one, yet in the New Testament it is represented as a special sin, and, as such, is to be distinguished from the more common sin of unbelief. The final sin of unbelief, moreover, may be judged, and will in the last day be judged, according to Matt. xxv, 41-46 and the Book of Revelation and elsewhere, by its fruits; and the sentence of the Judge will then be pronounced on the basis of these fruits. Unbelief damns under the Gospel, but unbelief will be judged according to its fruits of sin, as also faith, on the other hand, will be judged by its fruits.

These facts reveal to us the relation of the heathen to the Gospel, and to their final condemnation. They will not be condemned for what they have not, and cannot have, but alone for persistently and finally refusing the light given them in nature and the universal operations of the Holy Spirit. The cause of missions cannot expect to continue its appeals to the devotion and liberality of the Church on the ground of the indiscriminate damnation of the heathen simply for not having heard of Christ. Its appeal will hereafter be more rational, and true to the facts of Scripture.

"And there shall in no wise enter into it any thing that defileth, neither whatsoever worketh abomination, or maketh a lie: but they which are written in the Lamb's book of life."—Rev. xxi, 27.

CHAPTER V.

The Number of the Lost.

THE subject of the present chapter is one of the greatest importance. A false doctrine here would involve the gravest consequences; and it therefore becomes us to examine very closely as to the true teaching of the Scriptures concerning it.

In the writings of Universalists, and some others, it is quite generally assumed that the orthodox teaching includes the great mass of mankind among the damned. A few illustrative quotations will be in place. "I was, of course, immediately faced by the question, 'How can life be regarded as worth living by the majority of mankind if, as is taught by the current religious teaching, they are doomed to everlasting damnation?'" (Farrar, *Eternal Hope*, preface, p. xlvii. Dr. Pusey has culled thirteen passages from Dr. Farrar's little book in which similar expressions are used.) "Many are perplexed, hesitating to receive as perfect and divine a revelation which, they are told, in the name of God consigns a large proportion of those who in some sense at least are his offspring to everlasting misery" (Jukes, *Restitution of All Things*, preface, p. v). "Although the grounds on which these doctrines are alleged to rest differ widely from one another, the general conclusion which is deduced from them is for all practical purposes the same, namely, that Christianity affirms that the overwhelming majority of that innumerable multitude of men who have existed in the past and who exist in the present will, after this life is ended, pass into a state of endless existence in never-ending misery" (Row, *Future Retribution*, p. 2). "But when we consider the array of figures which would be required to represent the numbers of the human race who have existed in the past—according to the best computations more than twelve hundred millions exist in the present—and that those who, according to the above theories, will thus perish everlastingly will constitute an overwhelming majority of them, the thought is so awful that it may well set men thinking whether such theories can possibly be true" (*ibid.*, p. 16, *et passim*).

But this assumption is not true. The Christian Church does not teach that the majority of men will be lost. Over against the assumption we place the teaching of several of the most eminent advocates of the orthodox view. "A single remark remains to be made respecting the extent and scope of hell. It is only a spot in the universe of God. Compared with heaven hell is narrow and limited. The kingdom of Satan is insignificant in contrast with the kingdom of Christ. In the immense range of God's dominion good is the rule and evil is the exception. Sin is a speck upon the infinite azure of eternity; a spot on the sun. Hell is only a corner of the universe" (Shedd, *Dogmatic Theology*, vol. ii, p. 745). "We have reason to believe, as urged in the first volume of this work, and as often urged elsewhere, that the number of the finally lost in comparison with the whole number of the saved will be very inconsiderable. Our blessed Lord, when surrounded by the innumerable company of the redeemed, will be hailed as the *Salvator hominum*—the Saviour of men—as the Lamb that bore the sins of the world" (Hodge, *Systematic Theology*, vol. iii, p. 879). "As a final thought in eschatology, reference may be made to the vast preponderance of good over evil as the fruit of redemption and judgment. Not only will order be restored throughout the universe, but the good will far outnumber the bad; the saved will be many times more than the lost" (A. Hovey, *Biblical Eschatology*, p. 167). -" In respect, for example, to the number of the saved and of the lost, it is by no means just to allege with Farrar that, according to the position of orthodoxy, the latter class must include the vast majority of mankind" (E. D. Morris, *Is There Salvation After Death?* p. 235). "The race in its vast majority, the race as such, is actually saved [at the consummation of all things]; and as to the residue, it will be cast out not only from God, but from mankind, and not accounted of" (Pope, *Compendium of Christian Theology*, vol. iii, p. 428). "In the termination of the world's history the gospel of the kingdom shall be universally triumphant; that is, the mass of mankind shall be Christian believers and children of God, the few only remaining obstinate and rebellious" (Miner Raymond, *Systematic Theology*, vol. ii, p. 517). According to Shedd, even Calvin and Edwards believed the majority of mankind would be saved (*ut supra*, p. 747).

We now propose to examine the grounds of this larger view, and to consider certain passages of Scripture which seem to contradict it.

It must be confessed at the outset, however, that the question is a very difficult one, and one which does not easily admit of a categorical affirmative either one way or the other. One manifest reason is that it is a *contingent* question so far as responsible persons are concerned. Whether many or few will be saved depends wholly upon the willingness or final refusal of men to be saved. As to what will be the actual outcome, therefore, we cannot confidently know except by predictive revelation—a thing that is nowhere given.

It is very certain that no doctrine upon the subject can be based upon the comparative numbers in the parables of our Lord. In the parable of the Virgins *five* are wise and *five* foolish, but in that of the Talents the proportion of the faithful to the unfaithful is as *two* to *one*, and in the parable of the Wedding-garment (a parable within a parable) only *one* is cast out into the outer darkness (Matt. xxii, 11-14).

The words of our Lord in Matt. vii, 13, 14, 21-23; Luke xiii, 23-30, must be given in full: " Enter ye in by the narrow gate: for wide is the gate, and broad is the way, that leadeth to destruction, and many be they that enter in thereby. For narrow is the gate, and straitened the way, that leadeth unto life, and few be they that find it." "Not every one that saith unto me, Lord, Lord, shall enter into the kingdom of heaven; but he that doeth the will of my Father which is heaven. Many will say to me in that day, Lord, Lord, did we not prophesy by thy name, and by thy name cast out devils, and by thy name do many mighty works? And then will I profess unto them, I never knew you: depart from me, ye that work iniquity." "And one said unto him, Lord, are they few that be saved? And he said unto them, Strive to enter in by the narrow door: for many, I say unto you, shall seek to enter in, and shall not be able. When once the master of the house is risen up, and hath shut to the door, and ye begin to stand without, and to knock at the door, saying, Lord, open to us; and he shall answer and say to you, I know you not whence ye are; then shall ye begin to say, We did eat and drink in thy presence, and thou didst teach in our streets; and he shall say, I tell you, I know not whence ye are; depart from me, all ye workers of iniquity. There shall be the weeping and gnashing of teeth, when ye shall see Abraham, and Isaac, and Jacob, and all the prophets, in the kingdom of God, and yourselves cast forth without. And they shall come from the east and west, and from the north and south, and shall sit down in the kingdom of God. And behold, there are last which shall be first, and there are first which shall be last."

With regard to these passages we offer the following remarks: (1) "Many" will be cast out and lost. " Many will say to me in that day [certainly the last day, or day of judgment], Lord, Lord, did we not prophesy by thy name," etc. "And then will I profess unto them, I never knew you : depart from me [compare Matt. xxv, 41], ye that work iniquity." But this reveals nothing as to proportion; for "many" may be lost, and *more* saved. (2) On the other hand, the word "few" * is used but once in these passages by our Lord, and then in no unmistakable reference to the number of the finally saved. In Luke, where the questioner uses the word, Christ simply signifies that "many" will be lost, but does not say "few" will be saved. He certainly avoids a direct answer, and seems to intend: "Without saying any thing as to the number of the saved, *many* will be lost; therefore, strive *ye*

---

* The phrase, "For many are called, but few chosen," in Matt. xx, 16, is omitted in the Revised Version, and the same phrase in Matt. xxii, 14, has undoubted reference to the Jews. They were all called, but "few" of them accepted Christ. (See the whole parable, verses 1-14.)

to enter in by the narrow door." In Matt. vii, 14 (the instance where our Lord uses the word), is given a description simply of the state of things as Christ observed them. Few to whom the Gospel was offered accepted it. The same is true now. But this clearly says nothing as to the final outcome of life. Few are walking in the way that leads to life, but men may be saved in Christ in the last hour. Witness the familiar case of the thief on the cross. So many—the multitude—are walking in the way "that leadeth to destruction," but through grace may be, and no doubt many will be, saved at last. The way that *leadeth* to destruction is not itself destruction. In order to prove from this passage that the few only will be saved, it would be necessary to assume that to be lost *now* is to be lost forever.

In favor of the doctrine that the great majority of the human race will be saved may be urged:

1. The fact that children dying in infancy will be saved. Even Calvinists, as Dr. Hodge, now teach this doctrine. This writer says: "All who die in infancy are saved" (*Systematic Theology*, vol. i, p. 26). "The Scriptures nowhere exclude any class of infants, baptized or unbaptized, born in Christian or in heathen lands, of believing or unbelieving parents, from the benefits of the

redemption of Christ " (*ibid.*). To die in childhood is to such Calvinists a sign of election. " But we may still go a step further within the strict limits of the Reformed Creed, and maintain as a pious opinion that all departed infants belong to the number of the elect. Their early removal from a world of sin and temptation may be taken as an indication of God's special favor " (Schaff, *Creeds of Christendom*, vol. i, p. 380). From this teaching alone it follows that the majority of the human race will be saved, for the majority die before the age of accountability.

2. We cannot judge between the saved and the lost by a sharp line of moral distinction ; and, accordingly, many may be saved who by the standard of Christian morality manifest no sign of regenerate life. We have before pointed out this fact in relation to the heathen. The same may be said as to some persons in nominally Christian countries whose opportunities of moral improvement have been much limited. A few quotations in the line of this thought from several prominent writers will be in place:

" We are, then, wholly ignorant of the rule by which they [the heathen] will be judged. What would be heavy sin in us may be none in them ;

we cannot tell how far the exposure of infants may be a sin in China, unless God by his secret voice appeal to any individual parent against the hereditary custom, or cannibalism in a nation of cannibals. But since we are not God, and he has not bestowed on us his prerogative of searching the hearts, we have absolutely no ground upon which to form a judgment; nor do Christians form any.

"With the actual heathen far out of reach of the Gospel must be counted a large portion of the poor which the Church has lost in large cities, as London and Paris, on whose souls the light of the Gospel never shone. London is, alas! in all probability one of the largest heathen cities in the world, and very many of its inhabitants will be judged, we must suppose, by the same law as the heathen in China and Japan. 'God will,' in the great day, St. Paul says, 'judge the secrets of men by Jesus Christ according to my gospel.' The very terms forbid *our* judging, since they are the *secrets* of the heart which God will judge" (Pusey, *What is of Faith as to Everlasting Punishment?* pp. 9, 10. See the whole of this section and the following one, pp. 7-18).

"But if Abraham and Melchisedek, if Joseph and Moses, if Rahab and Cornelius, if a great number of the chosen people in every age may have been penitent for sin, and accepted by the Father of mercies through the atonement yet to be made, or an atonement already made without their knowledge, surely no one can deny the possibility of salvation to the heathen who know not the name of Jesus. Of course, no one is able to say how many of this class there have been among the heathen since the world began, or how many there may yet be before the end comes; but, whether few or many, all who are so renewed in the temper of their minds that they will recognize Christ whenever he is made known to them, as fulfilling all their desire and hope, will be numbered at the last great day with the redeemed " (A. Hovey, *ut supra*, p. 173).

"If the prayers and alms of Cornelius were had in divine remembrance—if in every nation he that feareth God and worketh righteousness is accepted of him—if our Lord heard the outcry of the dying thief, and carried him as a trophy at once into the paradise whither he himself was just going in triumph, may we not, without either indulging in the universalistic delusion or contradicting our own doctrine, still cherish with Pusey a large and comforting hope respecting many, perhaps multitudes, who live and die, alas! outside of the blessed circle of the Household of Faith?" (Morris, *Is There Salvation After Death?* p. 236.)

Is it not, we may ask, in connection with this doctrine that Christ's words concerning Tyre and Sidon and Sodom, and the two passages in First Peter, may be appropriately urged? We have seen that they cannot teach a future probation for the reason that in all cases the representations of mercy, however large, are concerning sins committed in this life alone. But we must confess we are not satisfied with the common interpretation of these passages, especially the two in First Peter. We cannot understand these latter passages, whatever more they may mean, to signify less than (1) That Christ in his disembodied condition went into the spirit-world; (2) That there he preached unto the "spirits in prison" the Gospel; (3) That the spirits to whom he preached, among others, were those who "were disobedient, when the long-suffering of God waited in the days of Noah, while the ark was a preparing." Can we believe all those people perished everlastingly after suffering the destruction of the flood? May we not rather believe, in view of the teaching of Peter, that many of them are saved *eternally*, while at the same time God could do no better than destroy them *temporally* ?

If we are to distinguish between the temporal destructions of *peoples* and the eternal destruction of *individuals*, it would seem that in the case of Tyre and Sidon and Sodom, and other ancient cities, many, perhaps multitudes, whose lives God destroyed with their cities will be saved in the day of the Lord Jesus. Nineveh was to be destroyed for its wickedness, and yet God said to Jonah that many of the people were so ignorant as to be unable to " discern between their right hand and their left hand " (chapter iv, 11). Can we suppose they would have been destroyed everlastingly with the destruction of their city, had Nineveh not repented? We cannot suppose so, and this case must throw light upon all similar cases ; and we must conclude that the inference involved here is the correct one.

3. The difficulties that we met in considering the doctrine of Universalism would be all the greater on the assumption that the majority of mankind will be lost. The divine love and foreknowledge, and the question of a benevolent teleology, would be all the more difficult to understand. We cannot believe the majority of the race of men will be lost, in view of these

facts, without the clearest revelation concerning it. This certainly is not given.

It is in this last respect that the present doctrine, in urging these facts, differs from Universalism when it urges the same; for in the case of the latter doctrine the revelation, as we have seen, is unmistakable.

4. For the same reasons we can the more consistently urge passages of Scripture like the following in favor of the doctrine we are considering: "He shall see of the travail of his soul, and shall be satisfied" (Isa. liii, 11); "Behold, the Lamb of God, which taketh away the sin of the world!" (John i, 29), etc. Such passages as these could not well have been inspired in the confident foreknowledge of the damnation of the majority of men.

Observe, however, we do not claim that such passages teach that the majority of men will be saved, but simply that, in the absence of a clear revelation that the majority will be lost, they encourage this hope.

We would remind the reader, in conclusion, that our chief concern with the present question should be, as Christ no doubt made it, *personal*. According to our Lord, as we have seen, "many" will be lost, and our fear should be lest we be among that number. "Strive to enter in by the narrow door: for many, I say unto you, shall seek to enter in, and shall not be able." " But I will warn you whom ye shall fear: Fear him, which after he hath killed hath power to cast into hell; yea, I say unto you, Fear him " (Luke xii, 5). " But I buffet my body, and bring it into bondage: lest by any means, after that I have preached to others, I myself should be rejected " (1 Cor. ix, 27).

"Knowing therefore the terror of the Lord, we persuade men."—2 Cor. v, 11.

"For our God is a consuming fire."—Heb. xii, 29.

CHAPTER VI.

The Nature of Future Punishment.

THE nature of future punishment is a question in itself of the greatest importance, and is not to be confounded with either of the other chief questions discussed in this book. We place it here as the most suitable time for its consideration. Its importance arises from several facts. 1. It is important that we should know, as fully as revealed, the nature of future punishment in order that the doctrine may have its proper influence upon the minds and hearts of men. It is in the nature of future punishment that the doctrine finds value as a deterrent from sin. 2. Its consideration is important, further, from the fact that its awfulness has been greatly exaggerated. The damnation of the lost is awful enough as represented in the Scriptures, without any human additions. 3. On the other hand, its terrors have been made largely to disappear by over-benevolent representations of it. Our aim shall be to present the doctrine in its true scriptural proportions.

As a matter of course, it is impossible to know the exact nature of future punishment except in the experience of it. It cannot be revealed. Consequently we find in the Scriptures only sensible and figurative representations of it. These are given under the following classified forms: 1. "Fire" and the "worm." "Where their *worm* dieth not, and the *fire* is not quenched" (Mark ix, 48). 2. "Outer darkness," or "blackness of darkness." "And cast ye out the unprofitable servant into the *outer darkness*" (Matt. xxv, 30). "For whom the *blackness of darkness* hath been reserved forever" (Jude 13; also 2 Pet. ii, 17). 3. 'Perishing," "destruction," "corruption," "death." "For God so loved the world that he gave his only begotten Son, that whosoever believeth on him should not *perish*" (John iii, 16). "Who shall suffer punishment, even eternal *destruction* from the face of the Lord and from the glory of his might" (2 Thess. i, 9). "For he that soweth unto his flesh shall of the flesh reap *corruption*" (Gal. vi, 8). "This is the second *death*, even the lake of fire" (Rev. xx, 14). 4. "Torment." "And he said, I pray thee therefore, father, that thou wouldest send him to my father's house; for I have five brethren; that he may testify unto them, lest they also come into this place of *torment*" (Luke xvi, 27, 28). "And they shall be *tormented* day and night for ever and ever" (Rev. xx, 10). 5. Other expressions suggestive of the terribleness of the state of the wicked are "cast away" and "lost." "But the bad they *cast away*" (Matt. xiii, 48). "For what is a man profited, if he gain the whole world, and *lose* or forfeit his own self" (Luke ix, 25). As a result of being excluded from heaven, we are told "there shall be *weeping* and *gnashing of teeth*" (Matt. xxv, 30).

Now, after allowing all we may be asked to allow for the natural exaggeration of Oriental hyperbole that may be found in these expressions, still we cannot but see in them the representation of a terrible reality for the wicked. "It is a fearful thing to fall into the hands of the living God" (Heb. x, 31). Two things seem perfectly clear: (1) The lost will be excluded from the presence of God, and the life and blessedness of the saved. Only the righteous shall have right to the tree of life, and shall be permitted to enter in by the gates into the city (Rev. xxii, 14). This is the negative side of the punishment of the lost, and has been called the penalty of loss (*pœna damni*), or absence of the beatific vision (*carentia beatificæ visionis*).

If this were all of hell we should seek diligently to escape it. But (2) it is also certain from the Bible representations of hell that the wicked will suffer a more positive penalty than is signified in these negative expressions. Such is implied in the word "torment" used in the parable of the Rich Man and Lazarus, and in Rev. xx, 10. This, however, is most likely itself the result simply of being without God, the source of our life and joy. The negative penalty of loss involves the positive penalty of pain (*pœna sensus*). The absence of the beatific vision creates the loneliness and desolateness of the soul that is "without God" and without "hope." The presence of darkness is but the absence of light, the presence of death but the absence of life.

This exclusion from the divine presence, with its negative and positive implications, may in-involve also remorse (Luke xvi, 25) and the evils of association with the damned (Rev. xxii, 15). It, of course, implies exclusion from the enjoyments of this life (Hodge).

We do not feel authorized to say less of the condition of the lost, nor need we say more.

We are, accordingly, obliged to think the following representations too mild to express the true sense of the Scriptures. "The will, in the exercise of its imperishable gift of freedom, may frustrate [the divine] education . . . ; but if it does so, it is because it 'kicks against the pricks' of the long-suffering that is leading it to repentance; and . . . it may accept even an endless punishment, and find peace in the acceptance" (Plumptre, *Spirits in Prison*, p. 340). "Thousands in this world are in conditions which other thousands pronounce worse than non-existence, but they themselves struggle hard and do their utmost to perpetuate their being—it may be through the fear of something worse, but more likely, in most cases, from an inherent natural love of conscious life. Sin may be declared to be exceeding sinful because it is offensive to God, whatever be its consequences to the sinner himself; and it is so again, because to the sinner it is a bar to the attainment of an infinite good, and is the source of an evil inconceivably great, even though it do not wholly overbalance the bliss of being" (Miner Raymond, *Systematic Theology*, vol. i, p. 357).

Such teaching, we are compelled to think, robs hell of its terrors, and contradicts the spirit and explicit representations of the Scriptures.

On the other hand, however, it is not necessary to go beyond the Scripture representations in the matter, and picture to ourselves a state of things more terrible than that revealed. The following doctrines, therefore, may be rejected as without warrant in the word of God:

1. That which represents the " fire " of hell as literal fire. Few only (as does Dr. Pusey) hold to this view to-day. The commoner view makes the fire of perdition symbolize the punishment of the lost.

Against the literal view may be urged: (1) The fact that if the " fire " must be considered literal, so also must the " worm ; " but these are incompatible. (2) The further representations of the state of the lost as given above are mutually exclusive on the basis of a literal interpretation. " Blackness of darkness " is not consistent with literal fire.

2. That which represents God as inflicting positive punishment. This is a very common view. To select one quotation out of a multitude, we may give the following : " Future suffering is not exclusively the natural consequence of sin, but also includes positive inflictions " (Hodge, *Systematic Theology*, vol. iii, p. 868).

We must ask the advocates of this view for the grounds of their assertion. We have not been able to find them.

3. Other excessive representations are all Dantean pictures of the condition of the lost. We know no warrant for such explorations and descriptions of the place and condition of the damned, and we certainly take no pleasure in such a task.

4. We know no sufficient warrant, moreover, for the assertion made by some, that the lost will have their bodies given to them in the resurrection in order to increase their sufferings. The statement is confessedly only an inference from the fact of their resurrection, and we should be extremely cautious of inferences upon a subject about which we know so little.*

But without being able to determine more precisely than we have the condition of the lost, we know from further Scripture representation that it is better for a man to pluck out a right eye, or cut off a right foot or arm, or to suffer the destruction of the whole body than to be cast into hell (Mark ix, 43, 45, 47; Luke xii, 4, 5); and that it were good for such an one as is cast therein if he had not been born (Matt. xxvi, 24).

---

* The ease with which some writers multiply their assertions upon this subject would suggest that they know much more about it than has been revealed. We know no part of our general subject where we should adhere more closely to the Scriptures than here; and yet because so little is revealed writers are no doubt all the more tempted to add their own conjectures.

"And these shall go away into everlasting punishment."—Matt. xxv, 46.

CHAPTER VII.

The Doctrine of Annihilation.

THE doctrine of the annihilation of the wicked is, in the nature of the case, opposed to the doctrine of Universalism. Its advocates strenuously oppose the latter error. They strongly advocate eternal punishment; not, however, as an eternal endurance, but in its results. If the wicked are annihilated, they say, their punishment is eternal in that its effects last forever. The doctrine, therefore, may properly be considered in connection with the subject of the nature of future punishment.

There are two forms of the doctrine—Annihilationism proper and the doctrine of Conditional Immortality, otherwise known as "life in Christ." The two doctrines are one in their outcome—the extinction of evil and evil-doers—but differ in other fundamental points. The chief points of difference concern the doctrine of native immortality and the method of ultimate annihilation. Annihilationism teaches that the soul was created immortal; Conditional Immortality teaches that it was created mortal, with the capacity of immortalization. Immortality is a gift of God in Christ. If sin had not entered into the world this gift would have been conferred (sacramentally, we suppose) through the "tree of life," from whose fruit our first parents were excluded after their fall. Christ is the new tree of life through whom, under grace, we again find access to immortality. In the view of this doctrine immortality is thus an acquisition, not an original endowment; and extinction of being is but the ultimate outcome of a responsible failure to obtain the life graciously offered to all in Christ. The other form of the doctrine, adhering to the metaphysical view that the soul is immortal by original constitution, teaches that its annihilation is by a divine destructive act corresponding to the divine creative act in its origination. In the doctrine of Conditional Immortality the soul dies of itself, ultimately, if without Christ; in the doctrine of Annihilation the soul that sinneth is ultimately destroyed; its immortality, being forfeited through sin, is, in the end, taken from it. Both doctrines teach a limited duration of conscious suffering for the wicked in the future life.

Such, in brief, is a doctrine in its twofold aspect, which (especially in the form of life in

Christ) is meeting with considerable favor in certain very respectable quarters; and we confess to a very strong liking for it. If our liking for a doctrine were all that we were required to consider we would find no difficulty in knowing where to cast the anchor of our faith. Both doctrines (especially the latter) have much in their favor. A divine theodicy is much easier under either view than under the orthodox doctrine. One of the heaviest burdens the latter doctrine is required to sustain is the eternal continuance of evil in a benevolent universe. Annihilationism does away with this difficulty by providing for the ultimate extinction of evil when the good and the pure and the happy will be " all in all," when sin shall no longer exist even as a " speck on the infinite azure of eternity," but when the last spot on the sun of righteousness shall be effaced. The doctrine (always especially the second form) is not wholly destitute of exegetical points. But when tested by the whole testimony of the Scriptures, we are compelled to believe that it is found wanting, and must, therefore, be rejected. We part from it as from a doctrine we would like to believe.

As the two forms of the doctrine readily classify in all essential respects, they may be considered together. We propose in the present chapter to review the chief grounds of the general doctrine.

1. The argument of the Annihilationist is based chiefly upon the use in the Scriptures of such words as "death," "destruction," "perishing," etc. To quote solely from the New Testament, some of the texts upon which much confidence is placed are as follows: "For the wages of sin is death" (Rom. vi, 23); "For if ye live after the flesh, ye must die" (*ibid.*, viii, 13); "And be not afraid of them which kill the body, but are not able to kill the soul: but rather fear him which is able to destroy both soul and body in hell" (Matt. x, 28); "Broad is the way that leadeth to destruction" (Matt. vii, 13); "For God so loved the world, that he gave his only begotten Son, that whosoever believeth on him should not perish, but have eternal life" (John iii, 16); "Who shall suffer punishment, even eternal destruction from the face of the Lord and from the glory of his might" (2 Thess. i, 9).

But we reply to the argument based upon such passages of Scripture, that these words are used in a figurative sense, and properly suggest simply the nature of eternal punishment. In proof of this assertion we offer the following facts: (1) The words "death," "destruction," etc., are used of persons in this life who are living in sin. The prodigal son, the "sheep," and the "piece of silver" were lost (destroyed), and Christ came "to seek and to save that which was lost [destroyed]*" (Luke xv, 3-7, 8-10, 24, 32; xix, 10). Men are, according to Paul, already "dead in trespasses and sins" (Eph. ii, 1, 5; Col. ii, 13), and "she that giveth herself to pleasure is dead while she liveth" (1 Tim. v, 6)—dead evidently to the higher life of righteousness and holiness. The prodigal son also was "dead" as well as "destroyed" (Luke xv, 24, 32). The morally and spiritually corrupt are the "dead" and the "destroyed," according to the New Testament; and the eternity of the finally lost is but the endless continuation of this state begun on earth, as the eternal life of the righteous is but the endless continuance of a life of holiness begun here. The Platonic use of these words in the sense of extinction of being is

* It is an unfortunate comment that Dr. Petavel (*Extinction of Evil*, p. 46) makes on these cases when he says: " But *for a time* the prodigal son was as good as lost [destroyed] to his father, and the coin as good as destroyed to its owner." Yes, we reply, as good as lost *to the father* and as good as destroyed *to the owner*, but not destroyed *in themselves*. The eternally lost are as good as destroyed to *their* Father, and worse than destroyed to themselves, but not annihilated.

not that of the New Testament. (2) The word "life" is used, correspondingly, with reference not simply to existence, but to a life of righteousness. There are several instances where the word cannot be made naturally to signify immortality. One of these is Rom. viii, 6 : "For the mind of the flesh is death; but the mind of the spirit is life and peace." Other instances are : "But godliness is profitable for all things, having promise of the life which now is, and of that which is to come" (1 Tim. iv, 8); "We know that we have passed out of death into life, because we love the brethren. He that loveth not abideth in death" (1 John iii, 14). Only an artificial interpretation can make either the word "death" or "life" in these passages signify more than a metaphorical condition of soul. (3) Confirmatory of the figurative interpretation of these terms is to be offered the fact that the New Testament repeatedly uses figurative expressions concerning the state of the soul. "Ye must be born again" (John iii, 7) is a familiar instance. Christ here did not mean that the soul needed to be brought into existence, but that it needed to be renewed in righteousness, and brought into the *life* of righteousness. (4) 2 Thess. i, 9, instead of furnishing evidence of annihilation, explicitly contradicts the annihilationist's use of the word "destruction." "Who shall suffer punishment, even eternal destruction from the face of the Lord and from the glory of his might." Here the meaning of the term "destruction" is defined in the subsequent part of the sentence. The destruction consists, evidently, according to the apostle, in the banishment of the soul from the presence of God and his glory. Nothing could be plainer than the meaning of Paul in this place. If he meant to teach the doctrine of Annihilation his language was wholly superfluous and meaningless. On the orthodox supposition his meaning is perfectly plain. (5) There are expressions in the New Testament which, by teaching eternal punishment, preclude the idea of annihilation. "And these shall go away into eternal punishment" (Matt. xxv, 46). "And they shall be tormented day and night for ever and ever" (Rev. xx, 10). (6) There are no instances of the use of the words in question where the orthodox view is not perfectly simple and intelligible.

2. But it is said in response that in the cases referred to, and all others like them, the words "death," "destruction," etc., though they in ordinary use properly signify annihilation, are used

proleptically. One writer, commenting on the phrase "dead in trespasses and sins," says: "We believe . . . that the apostle's statement means, 'Ye were [virtually] dead'—on your way to death. Death was there, though only in its germ ; death had begun its work, but was prevented from completing it. By prolepsis Paul anticipates the fatal results of total destruction, moral and physical, that sin would have wrought in his readers had they not received the Gospel" (Petavel, *Extinction of Evil,* p. 175). In confirmation of this view it is shown that prolepsis is a figure of speech sometimes used in the Scriptures. Instances are: "Whom he justified, them he also glorified" (Rom. viii, 30); "Death is swallowed up in victory" (1 Cor. xv, 54).

But we reply, while we grant that prolepsis is a true biblical figure of speech, we cannot admit the fact in this case. (1) The hypothesis is evidently devised not to meet a necessity in the use of New Testament language (this certainly, as before said, is intelligible and natural on the orthodox supposition), but to meet the exigency of a theory which cannot otherwise maintain itself. Prolepsis in the Scriptures we admit ; but to affirm this of language where there is no other necessity than the emergency of a foregone conclusion is not warrantable. When the advocates of annihilation can find one clear instance where the words " death," " lost," and the like, cannot signify, naturally and properly, spiritual degeneracy or the moral ruin of the soul, or when they on other grounds than these clearly establish their doctrine, then they may present their hypothesis of prolepsis as a demand of exegesis; not till then. And not till then will their doctrine carry conviction. (2) This meaning is not the natural impression that the language of the New Testament conveys to an unprejudiced reader. (3) It is contradicted by "4" and "5" above, in which we show that the apostle Paul defines his use of the word " destruction," and that Matt. xxv, 46, and Rev. xx, 10, expressly teach eternal suffering. (4) If we make the words " death " and " destruction " in the cases referred to signify a prolepsis, we must understand the word " life," when used with reference to the soul, in the same way. But we have seen that it cannot so refer in some cases. When Paul says, " Having promise of the life that now is," he evidently does not mean *existence*, but life in its higher worth and good. He does not mean more when he refers to "that [life] which is to come." In this case the metaphorical use

15

of "life" is not only perfectly natural; the sense of life as *immortality* is positively excluded.

3. Again, response is made to our objection from Matt. xxv, 46, and Rev. xx, 10, as follows: With regard to Rev. xx, 10, that no confidence is to be placed upon this for the reason that the Book of Revelation is a book largely of symbolisms, and theology, accordingly, can find only small ground in it to rest upon (Petavel, *ut supra*, p. 171). No less than six different attempts are made to avoid the manifest objection from Matt. xxv, 46. These are: (1) That κόλασις, (punishment) is not an absolutely certain reading of the original text. In proof of this is cited the fact that in certain manuscripts of the ancient Latin version of Matthew—the Itala—the word "fire" is found instead of "punishment," making the text read: "And these shall go away into eternal fire." It is assumed, of course, that "eternal fire" is not so strong an expression as "eternal punishment" (White, *Life in Christ*, p. 396; after him Row, *Future Retribution*, p. 268). (2) It is said that the word κόλασις itself suggests annihilation. "The etymology of the word *kolasis*, translated 'punishment' in the usual version, may lead us to an apprehension of its intrinsic meaning. Lexicographers refer it to a root signifying 'to break

by striking, to amputate, to shorten, to dismember, to mutilate;' from the said root our word *iconoclast*, 'breaker, or destroyer, of images,' is derived. *Kolasis*, therefore, denotes punishment involving a cutting off, a loss." It is said, in harmony with this, that all punishment involves loss. "A fine consists in loss of money; imprisonment, in loss of liberty; death, in loss of life" (Petavel, *Extinction of Evil*, p. 53). (3) It is said that the punishment of the wicked *is* eternal in its *results*, and that κόλασις αἰώνιος is to be understood in this sense after the analogy of such expressions as "eternal judgment" (Heb. vi, 2) and "eternal redemption" (Heb. ix, 12) (Petavel, pp. 33, 50). (4) Again, it is said that pain is not an essential part of punishment. "It is a mistake to think that punishment necessarily involves pain. . . . If any rash individual attempted to gaze at the sun, he would first experience intense pain in his eyeballs. Should he disregard the admonitory voice of suffering, and persevere, the pain would cease, but he would have become blind. The loss of sight would be his punishment, and not the temporary anguish that forewarned him of the consequences of his folly." "As instances of punishment without pain, we may quote the English law which condemned the suicide to an ignominious burial in the highway, with a stake driven through the body, and without Christian rites; also the custom prevalent in certain North American States of rendering criminals insensible by chloroform before their execution. Even without chloroform beheading and hanging are far less painful and terrible than many so-called natural deaths. If the essence of punishment were suffering, fifty lashes of the cat-o'-nine-tails would be a graver penalty than death on the scaffold, and murderers should be made to endure tortures proportionate to the number and atrocity of their crimes" (*ibid.*, pp. 56, 57). (5) It is also said that the word αἰώνιος does not signify everlasting (Row, *Future Retribution*, pp. 204–218). (6) When all of these devices fail, writers upon this subject quite generally warn us that we must not seek to build so great a doctrine as that of eternal suffering upon so slight a basis as one or two passages of the divine word; that this is like balancing "a mountain on the point of a needle," etc.

As to the first of these responses, we may say that while the Book of Revelation is confessedly a book largely of symbolisms, this does not affect the objection we urge from it to the present doctrine. The verse to which we refer, if it means any thing, clearly involves: 1.) The punishment of the devil after the judgment. 2.) Eternal punishment. We have already seen that the phrase εἰς τοὺς αἰῶνας τῶν αἰώνων is used to signify an intensified idea of eternity. 3.) Suffering as the essence of this eternal punishment. "Torment" can by no sort of exegetical legerdemain possibly be made to signify annihilation.

We may consider the other responses in their order.

(1) As to the reading of "fire" instead of "punishment." Even Dr. White does not urge this point as at all conclusive. "We shall, however, treat this passage on the supposition that . . . Matthew wrote what we find in these expressions" (*Life in Christ*, p. 396). It is only claimed that the reading "fire" is found in "the two most ancient, and several more modern, manuscripts of the Italic Version." This certainly can weigh nothing against the combined testimony of all the other versions and manuscripts. Besides, it is easier to see how the word "fire" could be interpolated in this verse by some transcriber than the word "punishment" (κόλασις), since "fire" (πῦρ) is used just before in verse 41. The transcriber who made the mistake had just

written πῦρ αἰώνιον. To make the mistake of writing κόλασις αἰώνιος a few verses after would have been wholly unnatural. But the mistake of writing πῦρ αἰώνιον in the second instance, as he had just written in the previous instance, was wholly natural and easy.

(2) The response that all punishment involves loss, and that this is signified in the word κόλασις. We reply, there can be no doubt that punishment involves loss, but not annihilation. Much less does it involve the annihilation of him who suffers it. It involves the loss of something to him, but not the loss of himself in the sense of extinction of being. To suffer a fine is to lose money, to suffer imprisonment is to lose liberty, to suffer death is to lose life; but this is not extinction in either case. As to the word κόλασις, we have already seen that it is used by the Universalist to establish his claim. It is used with as little plausibility by the Annihilationist. There can be no doubt whatever that the word, whatever its etymology, was used to signify punishment in general without reference to the mode or result of its infliction. The punishment (κόλασις) of Andronicus was by death (2 Macc. iv, 38). The Jewish authorities found " nothing how they might punish " the apostles

(Acts iv, 21). The word never signified annihilation.

(3) Eternal punishment is eternal in its effects. But this view will not explain Rev. xx, 10. Nor will it satisfy the spirit of the passage in Matthew. The whole structure of this sentence is well qualified to favor the orthodox view. "And these shall go away into eternal punishment." We cannot, except by forced construction, make this mean : "And these shall be finally annihilated." The *going away into* eternal punishment is just such language as might have been used by our Lord to signify eternal suffering. Moreover, this is its common impression upon an unprejudiced reader. Again, the Annihilationist no more than the Universalist can explain the contrasted phrases in this verse. There is no more reason, except through the exigency of a foregone conclusion, to say "eternal punishment" means the eternal result of temporal suffering than to say "eternal life" means the eternal result of a temporal existence. The two phrases are evidently intended parallels, and their unforced impression will forever witness against both the Annihilationist and Universalist hypotheses. Further, the Annihilationist himself concedes that this phrase does not mean the

eternal result of a single act, as in the analogous cases cited, where "eternal judgment" means the eternal result of an act of judgment and "eternal redemption" the eternal result of the atonement; for he teaches a *gradual* extinction of the lost. They go away into a punishment that will ultimately be annihilation. Still further, in the analogous cases the context *compels* the secondary construction; not so in this. Lastly, the Jews of Christ's time, who, as we have seen, taught eternal suffering for some, and who also taught annihilation for others, did not use language like that in question to signify the second doctrine. In regard to sinners of Israel the School of Hillel taught " that they are tormented in Gehenna for twelve months, after which their bodies and souls are burnt up and scattered as dust under the feet of the righteous ; but it significantly excepts from this number certain classes of transgressors ' who go down to Gehinnom and are punished there to ages of ages' " (Edersheim, *Life and Times of Jesus the Messiah*, vol. ii, p. 792). In view of this teaching, and the language used to convey it, there is no way of mistaking the language of our Lord.

(4) The response which affirms that pain is not an essential part of punishment. This, we reply,

is a contradiction in terms. There is no punishment without pain of some kind. To be sure it need not be physical pain; this, indeed, is not always the severest. The supposed cases of painless punishment referred to by Dr. Petavel are not apt instances. Is there no pain to a man who by a rash act destroys his eyesight except that which is experienced in the act? Will he not *suffer* from the loss of his eyesight as long as he lives? As to the English law that condemned the suicide to an ignominious burial in the highway with a stake driven through his body, this can only be said to be punishment to the offender in an accommodated sense. It was an example to others, and if properly a punishment to the guilty one, only so in its anticipation. In this latter sense it was punishment to the suicide, and only as such could it have any deterrent effect upon others. The pain experienced in the thought of this ignominious burial was what gave it its deterring force, if it had any, and what properly constituted its penalty. Again, is there no pain in being hung even if the criminal is rendered insensible by an anæsthetic? Is there not pain in the thought of dying the felon's death? And if there is greater suffering in the lash of the cat-o'-nine-tails than in death on the scaffold, and the murderer deserves the worst form of punishment of the two, why, in the name of common-sense, not give him the punishment of the former and save him from the latter? It will take Dr. Petavel a long time to persuade the world that there is more suffering in the first than in the last.

We do not teach that there is conscious eternal suffering in all punishment, but simply that suffering is an essential element of all punishment; and that "eternal punishment" involves eternal suffering.

(5) The Annihilationist as well as the Universalist seeks to prove that αἰώνιος does not signify "everlasting." Enough, however, has been said upon this point in considering the doctrine of the latter.

(6) As to building the doctrine of future suffering upon a few passages of Scripture. In this objection the Annihilationist practically surrenders his doctrine. It is a virtual confession that a few passages of Scripture teach the orthodox view. Again, how many times was it necessary for our Lord to say, " And these shall go away into eternal punishment," in order to convince these writers that he meant to teach this doctrine? A thousand times would not more perfectly teach it than this once, although repetition em-

phasizes. But this is accomplished in the use of other language, as that which the Annihilationist himself urges, and by the whole implication of the gospels. We have tried to set forth the full impression of this doctrine in the first chapter.

4. The Annihilationist seeks to augment his argument based upon the terms " death " " destruction," and the like, by such Scriptures as the following: "If a man abide not in me, he is cast forth as a branch, and is withered ; and they gather them, and cast them into the fire, and they are burned" (John xv, 6). "And if thy hand cause thee to stumble, cut it off: it is good for thee to enter into life maimed, rather than having thy two hands to go into hell, into the unquenchable fire " (Mark ix, 43). It is said fire " symbolizes total destruction." It is also the agent of the destruction of the wicked. " Fire changes the diamond, the hardest of all substances, into a subtle vapor, dissolves granite and converts it into lava. . . . No sort of life is compatible with fire ; and, according to the Bible, destruction by fire is the doom of the ungodly ; ' for, behold, the day cometh, that shall burn as an oven ; and all the proud, yea, and all that do wickedly, shall be stubble : and the day that cometh shall burn them up, saith the Lord of

hosts, that it shall leave them neither root nor branch'" (Petavel, p. 44).

But it will not be claimed that these passages can teach the doctrine if those already considered do not. Besides, there is no more reason, as already seen in a previous chapter, for affirming that the "fire" threatened the sinner is a literal fire than that the "worm" and the "outer darkness" are literal—incompatible representations. All of these are but sensible and figurative representations used to signify the character of future suffering.

5. The Annihilationist seeks to build his doctrine from the positive side upon the word "life" as used in the New Testament. Life, he says, is immortality, as "death" is extinction. This life is in Christ. It will not be necessary to quote passages in which this word is found, as the reader by consulting his concordance can readily find access to many of them. Nor will it be necessary to respond to the argument based upon them at any great length, since the interpretation of this word stands or falls with what has already been said concerning "death" and its kindred words. We simply desire to reiterate one or two remarks before made. One of these is that there is no instance of the use of the word "life" in

the New Testament that is not compatible with the orthodox interpretation. The other is that the word is so used in some instances as positively to exclude the connotation of immortality. We quote other instances than those given. "And he said unto them, Take heed, and keep yourselves from all covetousness: for a man's life consisteth not in the abundance of the things which he possesseth" (Luke xii, 15). "Jesus therefore said unto them, Verily, verily, I say unto you, Except ye eat the flesh of the Son of man and drink his blood, ye have not life in yourselves. He that eateth my flesh and drinketh my blood hath eternal life; and I will raise him up at the last day. For my flesh is meat indeed, and my blood is drink indeed. He that eateth my flesh and drinketh my blood abideth in me, and I in him" (John vi, 53–56). What more reason to interpret "life" here literally than to interpret "flesh" and "blood," as do the Romanists, in the same way? "Again therefore Jesus spake unto them, saying, I am the light of the world: he that followeth me shall not walk in darkness, but shall have the light of life" (John viii, 12). If we cannot interpret "light" and "darkness" literally, why should we interpret "life" so in this verse? "The thief cometh not, but that he may steal, and kill, and destroy: I come that they may have life, and may have it abundantly" (John x, 10). Suppose we understand the word "life" here to signify immortality, what will be the result upon the sense of this passage? It would then read: "I come that they may have immortality, and may have it abundantly." Will the literalist tell us what an *abundance* of immortality is? By his interpretation the sense of the passage is destroyed. There are degrees of spiritual life and righteousness in Christ, but not degrees of immortality.

6. Argument is attempted by the Annihilationist from considerations of the divine love and justice. These coincide perfectly with the same as presented by the Universalist, and have been sufficiently considered in refuting the doctrine of the latter.

7. It is said that native and inamissible immortality is not revealed in the Bible; that the doctrine is borrowed from Plato and not derived from the Scriptures. It is said further to be positively opposed by the Scriptures. The two chief passages upon which reliance is placed in proof are Gen. iii, 4, 22–24, and Rom. ii, 7. It is said, according to the former passage immortality was conditioned upon the tree of life. As to

the second, it is said that God "only hath immortality" (1 Tim. vi, 16), and that we attain it by seeking it. Again, it is said that "enforced" immortality is contrary to the teaching of "universal analogy." "All about us in the world we behold a struggle for existence and the survival of the fittest. Be transformed in order to live! Such is the great law of nature. Such is also the great law of the Gospel. What, from this point of view, shall befall those free beings who resist the required transformation and, in lieu of progressing, recoil voluntarily and obstinately toward animalism? Evolutionary science itself exhibits examples of retrogression in nature, degenerations, backward progress. Without culture superior types revert to the primitive type. The conscious being may revert toward the unconscious, and in fact the sleep which takes possession of each of us every day is like the daily menace of this unconsciousness from which we have scarcely emerged" (*Extinction of Evil*, p. 96). We are told, still further, that we are to distinguish, according to the Scriptures, between the soul's survival of death and the resurrection and its inamissible immortality. "I have also drawn the reader's attention to the fact that two questions which ought to be kept entirely distinct have been habitually confounded together in this controversy. One of these is, Have we reason for believing that man will survive the dissolution of the body? the other, Will that survival be of endless duration?" (C. A. Row, *Future Retribution*, p. 408).

To all of this we respond in order.

(1) Immortality not revealed. To this we reply, not only is the immortality of the soul every-where assumed in the Scriptures, as is the existence of God, but it is also involved in the fact of eternal punishment as already proved by the Scriptures. Again, it is involved in Christ's conversation with the Sadducees recorded in Matt. xxii, 23-33; Mark xii, 18-27; Luke xx, 27-40 : " And there came to him certain of the Sadducees, they which say that there is no resurrection ; and they asked him, saying, Master, Moses wrote unto us, that if a man's brother die, having a wife, and he be childless, his brother should take the wife, and raise up seed unto his brother. There were therefore seven brethren : and the first took a wife, and died childless ; and the second ; and the third took her ; and likewise the seven also left no children, and died. Afterward the woman also died. In the resur-

rection therefore whose wife of them shall she be? for the seven had her to wife. And Jesus said unto them, The sons of this world marry, and are given in marriage : but they that are accounted worthy to attain to that world, and the resurrection from the dead, neither marry, nor are given in marriage: for neither can they die any more: for they are equal unto the angels; and are sons of God, being sons of the resurrection. But that the dead are raised, even Moses showed, in the place concerning the Bush, when he calleth the Lord the God of Abraham, and the God of Isaac, and the God of Jacob. Now he is not the God of the dead, but of the living: for all live unto him. And certain of the scribes answering said, Master, thou hast well said. For they durst not any more ask him any question." Now there can be no reasonable doubt that Jesus in this conversation took the side of the Pharisees, who believed in the resurrection and the immortality of the soul, against the Sadducees, who believed in neither (Acts xxiii, 8). It is a pure assumption to affirm, as does Dr. White, that Christ contradicted the doctrine of the Pharisees in this matter as well as that of the Sadducees. The well-known positions of these two parties among the Jews (and there was no middle party) makes it certain that Christ's unqualified approbation of the doctrine of the Pharisees in this conversation with the Sadducees implies his approval of the former's doctrine of the native immortality of the soul. If Jesus had meant to teach a doctrine neither of the Pharisees nor Sadducees, but one midway between the two, he certainly would not have used the language that he did without guarding it against the doctrine of the former. The fact furnishes as clear ground for the inference that Jesus assumed the native immortality of the soul as should be desired.

(2) The Scriptures opposed to native immortality. As to the passage in Genesis urged to prove this, we reply that it can be of force only on the assumption that "to die" meant to be annihilated. But this would be begging the whole question, for it is just this point that is in dispute. There certainly is no more difficulty in supposing the tree of life to be able to conserve physical and spiritual life than in supposing it able to impart immortality. In either case it could only have possessed this power sacramentally; and there is nothing in the narrative itself to lead us to suppose that its office was to impart immortality except we assume that man

was created mortal—the very thing, as just said, in question. Besides, when it is remembered, as already remarked, that the immortality of the soul is every-where assumed in the Scriptures—Old and New—it becomes impossible to interpret the narrative in question according to the peculiar view of the doctrine of conditional immortality. As to the passage in Romans we need only say that it is to be understood to signify a *blessed* immortality.* Analogous to this use of the word ἀφθαρσία (the word used in this place, and translated " incorruption " in the Revised Version) is its use in the Septuagint. (See *Greek-English Lexicon of the New Testament*, Thayer.) Besides, all the other facts in the case necessitate this interpretation, and no violence is thereby done to the passage.

(3) The argument from analogy. We have little to do with this argument except to refer to it, for the reason that a skillful writer can find proof from the so-called analogy of nature for any doctrine that he undertakes to prove. We

---

* There can be no doubt that the Greek words ἀφθαρσία (the word in Rom. ii, 7, and translated "incorruption" by our revisers) and ἀθανασία (translated alike in the Authorized and Revised Versions by our word "immortality") are used synonymously in the New Testament. Examine 1 Cor. xv, 53, 54; 1 Tim. i, 17.

are abundantly persuaded that analogy can serve safely only two functions, namely, that of *illustration*, and to remove objections to doctrines involved in difficulties. Even Butler, the great master in this field, strikes us as strong only where he seeks to remove objections to the doctrines he considers.*

(4) Survival does not involve immortality according to the Scriptures. But we assert directly the contrary. The Scriptures nowhere make the distinction between survival and immortality. This is a distinction devised, like the doctrine of prolepsis, to meet the peculiar emergency of this doctrine. Its advocates had need of it, and they created it. This will be evident when it is remembered that no such distinction was ever made outside of the Scriptures. Both in ancient and modern times it has been customary to argue for the immortality of the soul as if this were involved in the survival of the soul in the dissolution of the body. Unless it can be shown that the Bible explicitly departs from this custom the alleged distinction

---

*An example of both the weakness and the strength of the argument from analogy has lately appeared in Drummond's *Natural Law in the Spiritual World*—a book weak in its fundamental principle (the identity of natural and spiritual law), but strong in its apt and beautiful illustrations.

will fall to the ground. But this cannot be shown.

From purely exegetical considerations, therefore, we are compelled to reject the present doctrine; and simply say, in conclusion, that the convictions of men in all ages and parts of the world concerning the soul's native immortality are not lightly to be set aside. We do not seek to base our doctrine upon this primarily; nor upon metaphysical considerations of the soul's immortality. These could weigh nothing in our view against the clear teaching of the Scriptures to the contrary; but finding the doctrine assumed every-where in the Scriptures, we may find confirmation of it in these extra-biblical facts and arguments. We see no reason, moreover, in the metaphysical nature of the soul (this being granted) to prevent its annihilation. He who created it is able to destroy it; but this also is not revealed, but the contrary.

"For the wrath [justice] of God is revealed from heaven against all ungodliness and unrighteousness of men, who hold the truth in unrighteousness"—Rom. i, 18.

"Just and true are thy ways, thou King of saints."—Rev. xv, 3.

CHAPTER VIII.

The Reason or Law of Necessity in Future Punishment.

WE have now sufficiently considered the fact and nature of future punishment. One other task yet remains, namely, to investigate the reason or law of necessity in the punishment of the lost. Why must the wicked be punished forever?

This is, perhaps, the least important part of our subject, and yet it is not without interest, and its consideration will not be without value. Several chapters might be devoted to its discussion, but we prefer to embrace it within the compass of a single chapter.

Any proposed solution of the problem that deserves so much as a hearing must begin by taking for granted some *real* necessity; and not, as in Calvinism, by making the fact of punishment the result of divine caprice. Excluding the answer of Calvinism, and postulating some deep necessity, we inquire wherein that necessity lies.

1. Is it in fixation of character? This is a well-known doctrine, and is found in much of

the current teaching upon the subject. Its fundamental principle is that character, by the constant and long indulgence of sin, becomes so confirmed in badness that it bears in itself its own unalterable, and therefore necessary, doom. Thus Mr. Joseph Cook says:

"I did not make the universe; but the universe is so made that whoever sins against light draws blood on the spiritual retina of the moral eyes. It is the most mysterious thing in the penalties the soul is called on to endure, that sinning against light blinds us to the very illumination needed to rectify our condition. That is a fact of science; that is a terrific philosophical truth which cannot be declaimed out of sight; that is a tremendous, indisputable circumstance in natural law; and on it I plant myself when I say reason shows that resisting the light that comes in death may fix character and so end probation" (*Boston Monday Lectures: Occident*, p. 59).

Of course, whatever ends probation is itself the law of necessity in eternal punishment. So Mr. Cook would have us understand; and on the ground of the fixed character would he exclude repentance after death, and justify to human reason the compatibility of eternal punishment with divine benevolence.

Certainly it would follow, if the doctrine were true, that there could be no repentance after death, and no blame could be cast upon divine goodness ; but, however plausible and convenient the theory may appear, when tested by the Scriptures it is found to be untenable. Several facts will demonstrate its untenableness:

(1) *All* character is fixed without helping grace. This fact will not be disputed by any one ; but it is lost sight of in its bearing upon the doctrine under discussion. The theory of Mr. Cook tacitly assumes that no character is fixed but that which becomes so from long and habitual sinning; whereas, as just said, all character is unalterably fixed without the intervention of divine grace. Under the economy of redemption the Holy Ghost is the light that lighteth every man that cometh into the world, so that no character is left to its naturally fixed condition of moral impotency in the beginning ; but we must carefully remember that the reason of this moral or spiritual strength is in the presence and power of the Holy Spirit. If for any reason the Holy Spirit should take his flight from us, character would be forever sealed in ruin from our consequent weakness or inability to reform.

It is true, as Mr. Cook maintains, that character under sin becomes less and less susceptible to appeals of religious truth; "that sinning against light blinds us to the very illumination needed to rectify our condition:" but why? The answer of the fixation doctrine is, Because character by sin becomes more and more hardened, and, therefore, less and less susceptible to the influence of the Holy Ghost, who alone can apply truth to the hearts of men in conviction and salvation. Thus Mr. Cook again:

"I believe that light is kept before the lost. I believe that God will be all in all both in the saved and in the lost, and that the fact that God is all in all in a lost soul is the chief source of its misery" (*Occident*, p. 67).

This is the natural conclusion of the doctrine as applied in its outcome to the future life. The Holy Spirit is ever present, but finds its inability for good in the moral steadfastness of the lost soul. It ever strives to save, but is debarred by the soul's fixedness in evil.

How obviously contradictory is this to those passages of Scripture which signify the withdrawal of the Holy Ghost on account of sin and imply the moral ruin of the soul from that withdrawal? "Cast me not away from thy presence; and take not thy Holy Spirit from me" (Psa.

li, 11). "And grieve not the Holy Spirit of God, in whom ye were sealed unto the day of redemption" (Eph. iv, 30). Here the danger is not that the character will become so fixed by sin that the Holy Spirit cannot influence it, but that the Holy Ghost will cease its wooing and leave the soul to its natural state of ruin. As sinning tends to drive the Holy Spirit from us, we infer that in proportion as its influence grows less on account of our sins are we less and less susceptible to appeals of religious truth. As we become hardened to religious impressions on account of the Spirit's gradual but sure withdrawal on account of sin, it follows that when the Spirit ceases to operate upon the heart there is then no further hope of moral or religious good. Left alone, man's character is forever sealed in ruin. Why the Holy Spirit finally ceases to strive with rebellious man will be seen when we come to consider the theory which gives the true account of the necessity in eternal punishment. Why the Holy Spirit gradually leaves the sinful in this life may be accounted for on the ground of his willful rejection. The Holy Ghost cannot trespass upon free moral agency. It is an awful fact, significant of man's greatness in the scale of being, that at the bidding of a human will the Holy Spirit must retire. He cannot, as well as will not, stay unwelcomed and forbidden.

What has been said at this point may be summed up for the sake of clearness and emphasis as follows: All character is unalterably fixed without prevenient grace; the light of the Holy Spirit, which lighteth every man that cometh into the world, makes moral and spiritual reform possible; and the final withdrawal of that Spirit on account of sin forever fixes lost character because left to its natural condition of moral and spiritual helplessness. The fixation doctrine, which assumes the reverse of this, namely, that the Spirit is ever present, but debarred from helpfulness on account of fixed character, cannot, therefore, be true.

(2) Again, it is pure assumption to affirm that character can become so fixed as to be beyond the possibility of grace to reclaim, *all other considerations aside*. There is not a passage in the Bible which teaches such a doctrine or warrants such a conclusion. There are passages that are quoted as proof-texts, but they by no means prove it. A favorite passage is Gal. vi, 7, 8: " Be not deceived; God is not mocked: for whatsoever a man soweth, that shall he also reap.

For he that soweth unto his own flesh shall of the flesh reap corruption; but he that soweth unto the Spirit shall of the Spirit reap eternal life." That this passage teaches certain natural consequences to a life of sin and others to a life of righteousness, which it names, is not in the least disputed; but it does not, therefore, teach that in steadfastness of character is to be found the reason or law of eternal punishment. The conclusion goes beyond the teaching of the text, or any warrantable inference from it. The error in the interpretation here, and in the inference as to the future life that is drawn from it, as in that of other passages of similar import, is in the failure to make the proper distinction between fixity of character as the inevitable result of a sinful life whose probation is ended, where by implication and in fact there is no reclaiming or restraining grace, and fixity of character as the reason or law of eternal punishment. As all character without prevenient grace is unalterably fixed, so when man persistently refuses the assistance of divine grace his character becomes more and more confirmed in badness. And so it is that all lost character is eternally fixed. This much of the theory is fundamentally true; but we believe it is true, not because grace has not the power to rescue, but because a limitation, outside of the lost soul, is placed upon the working of that grace. What that limitation is will be seen presently. In the meantime let it be borne in mind that fixity of character as a *result* of being left alone and as a *law explaining the necessity of eternal punishment* are radically different.

(3) Another fatal objection to the theory is that it necessarily implies, and therefore assumes, if it does not assert, that the relations and conditions of the future life of the lost are substantially the same as those of this life. But there is one important difference which must never be forgotten, namely, the momentary gratification from sin in this life cannot be received there. This inference is in harmony with all Scripture teaching with regard to the lost. We must not forget that men in this life would not risk and suffer the consequences of sin were it not for the momentary pleasure of present indulgence. It is inconceivable, therefore, that a free will can attain such an "ultimate steadfastness and unchanging bent" that it will eternally choose the "torment" of hell in the absence of pleasurable gratification. We might conceive how in a life such as this, as long, at least, as the sen-

sations of pleasure were possible, a corrupted heart and perverted will might choose the evil; but not in a life such as the future of the wicked will be, where all the conditions and opportunities of sinful pleasure are past. Conceivably, will not the punishment of the wicked goad them, at least, to a desire of deliverance? If, like the rich man, they be driven by the burnings to call for a drop of cold water, who will say that the Spirit could not send that drop, and even take them out of the flame, were there no barrier outside of themselves? Might not that Spirit that changes the heart of stone to a heart of flesh in this life even change the hardened character of the lost were there no other law that places a limit upon its operation? The "great gulf fixed" is *between* the saved and the lost, and not *in* the lost.

(4) Still further, and of great and conclusive significance, is the fact that the Scriptures everywhere represent eternal punishment as a judicially inflicted penalty, and not as the natural result of a sinful life. All those passages which speak of the wrath of God as revealed from heaven against all ungodliness and unrighteousness of men, and, as well, those which describe the final judgment, proclaim the truth and validity of this

objection. Moreover, all the terms used with reference to the matter are of a judicial nature. "Judge," "judgment," "punishment," are familiar scriptural examples. Christ, in Matt. xxv, 33, is represented as a judge pronouncing judicial sentence upon the good and the bad for acts in life, and not as one declaring to men the natural results of their earthly conduct. If the doctrine of fixity of character were true, we might expect to find in the Bible no threatened penalties, but only warning as to natural consequences. It should be observed that the sin against the Holy Ghost has never *forgiveness*. Christ does not say: "But he that shall blaspheme against the Holy Ghost will attain final permanence of character that can never be changed," or any thing like it; and any interpretation that reads it so forces into the Saviour's words, not only a meaning that they do not contain, but one that is contradictory to their judicial sense.

(5) Lastly, it may be asked, if this doctrine be true, how account for an atonement in any true sense of atonement, as a plan to deliver from the eternal penalties of sin? If fixation of character is the only bar to final restoration, then what need of an atonement for forgiveness? A

moral influence atonement is, on supposition of this doctrine, the only atonement needed; for, clearly, all that men need is remedy, not forgiveness; unless we assume that forgiveness through the atonement is of sins with only temporal guilt. Clearly, the atonement that makes possible the remission of eternal guilt teaches that there is a barrier other than fixation of character that precludes the restoration of the lost, who have rejected that atonement, to holiness and heaven.

The nature of eternal punishment is not under consideration; yet it should be said that possibly this is to be understood as being in the burnings of an unalterably fixed evil character; which fixity of character, as explained, is the result of being left alone by divine grace. Divine justice may judicially surrender a lost soul to the eternal gnawings and burnings of a bad character. The judicial act would thus be the surrendering; the punishment, the result of that surrender, which, in any case, would be moral and spiritual destitution. This, at least, seems to be the doctrine of Rev. xxii, 11. In these awful words sound forth both the eternal sentence of the Judge and the eternal doom of the wicked, as well as the eternal lot of the righteous. Moreover, the term "death"

17

as used in the New Testament to signify the lost condition of the wicked, and which is, therefore, equivalent to "everlasting punishment"—the opposite of "life eternal"—seems to teach the same doctrine. Eternal death is not in the extinction or annihilation of the soul, but in the total loss of the divine holiness and presence, as eternal life is the eternal life of God in the soul. In this deprivation of the life of God, which must be eternal death, is to be found, it would seem, the nature of that punishment to which the justice of God surrenders the finally impenitent. Here, if anywhere in connection with this doctrine, might be appropriately quoted Gal. vi, 7, 8, and similar Scriptures, with their inferential significance.*

---

* Since this chapter was written we have met a doctrine the very reverse of the one just reviewed. It is the doctrine of Dr. Campbell's little book, *Unto the Uttermost*. It rejects the fixation doctrine, and, taking its suggestion, it would seem, from *Dorner* (vol. iv, p. 424), makes the only barrier in the way of final universal restoration to consist in the eternal and free refusal of the soul to be restored. Thus: "The freedom of man as a moral being, and his consequent responsibility to God, continue forever under conditions which render response to every moral requirement eternally possible" (Preface, *et passim*). But this is to remove every barrier to universal restoration, for no soul can choose eternal hell. The *Andover Review* rightly designates the book of Dr. Campbell as "Restorationist."

2. Is the law of necessity in eternal punishment from eternal sinning?

"It is not that the Judge assigns eternal punishment for temporal sin; but that sin is taken confirmed into eternity. *Non cessante peccato nequit cessare pœna.* It is not because man has sinned only, but because his nature is turned away from God, and he sins still. One of our Lord's most solemn words of threatening prediction was this: 'Ye shall die in your sins'" (*Pope's Compendium of Christian Theology*, vol. iii, p. 421). "There is no eternal punishment but of eternal sinning: the eternal state of separation from God is both sin and its punishment" (*ibid.*, 437).

The following is taken from *The Christian Advocate* of October 23, 1884, in an article entitled "Eternal Sinning," by Rev. T. H. Armstrong, Ph.D. :

"But these are held in eternal sin; such is the habit they have fixed about themselves that they cannot but sin. Each new day of eternity the soul will darken with sin and discharge upon itself the wrathful shafts of the nature of things. The righteous Judge does not assign eternal punishment for temporal sin, but that sin is taken confirmed into eternity. Well has one of the fathers said : *Non cessante peccato nequit cessare pœna*. While sin does not cease it is impossible for punishment to cease. It is the sin which the soul commits in eternity for which it shall be punished eternally, and not the sin of this probationary life. Until some one can show how the soul can be delivered from sin in eternity, eternal punishment cannot be denied."

A composite doctrine, it starts with assuming eternal fixedness of character as the ground of eternal sinning, and awards the punishments —not *punishment*—of eternity to the lost on the ground of eternally repeated acts of sinning.* Thus Christ will be forever a Judge awarding to the lost the just penalties of their continual sins! Or, perhaps, the eternity of punishment will be awarded in the judgment once for all in view of the foreseen eternal sinning! Moreover, eternal punishment is not the penalty for sins committed " in the body " (2 Cor. v, 10); but the punishments of eternal sinning *out of the body*.

The manifestly anti-scriptural character of this

---

* In Dr. Pope's treatment of the doctrine a *state* is said to be sin (a doctrine that well accords with the equally untenable doctrine of "hereditary guilt"); and for this guilty state the punishment of eternity is awarded.

doctrine makes it unnecessary to notice it further.*

3. We may now turn to a theory which is thoroughly scriptural, and answers, as we believe, to a real necessity. It is the doctrine of the Methodist Catechism.

Question.—" Why is it right and necessary that God should punish sin?"

Answer.—" In order to vindicate his law, to preserve his authority, and to promote the greatest good of his creatures" (Catechism No. 3, p. 28).

The doctrine thus succinctly stated finds its fundamental principles in the Scriptures, and bases its conclusions on those principles. The following propositions are, therefore, quite self-evident.

(1) God is a moral Ruler; and as such has established certain laws of his government, and affixed penalties to those laws as their sanction.

(2) The honor of God and the good of his obedient moral subjects are involved in the conservation of his government.

(3) Without penalty law could not restrain the

---

*Perhaps attention might well be called to the fact that he who commits the sin against the Holy Ghost is said to be " guilty of an eternal sin " (Mark iii, 29).

disobedient; for such law, if indeed it can properly be called law, would be no more than entreaty or advice.

(4) Without law there could be no moral government over free intelligent beings.

(5) Without government there would be anarchy in the moral universe.

(6) God as a God of justice, as well as a God of love, could not allow anarchy to prevail among his intelligent moral subjects; for that would be indifference to the interests of those whose choice is that of obedience and holiness.

(7) God, having created free moral subjects, and having established the principles of moral government, is bound—but bound by a *self-imposed* obligation*—to conserve his government

---

* It is objected to this doctrine by some that it ties the hands of God, and is, consequently, a reflection upon the divine almightiness. Our reply is, Even creation is a limitation upon God; and natural law as much so as governmental law. The limitation of creation (in which is involved that of natural law), which Pantheism urges as an objection to Theism, is, as Dr. G. P. Fisher says, "voluntary. It is a *self-limitation*," and "a most free act, performed in the exercise of benevolence." The same is our defense of the divine governmental limitations. Moreover, governmental laws inhere in, or are based upon, the nature of moral relations. Moral law is by reason of created moral beings, and upon the fact and ground of moral law is superinduced governmental law; so that the divine governmental law is founded upon so-called natural law; or, in other words, upon divinely established natural relations. Besides, it

for his own honor and the interests of his obedient subjects.

(8) The penalty that God has affixed to his laws as their sanction is eternal punishment.

(9) The only escape from that penalty for guilty man is in the atonement.

(10) The atonement rejected in probation leaves the soul after death to the endurance of the penalty of God's violated laws.*

This is a brief statement of principles which need no elaboration.

All that was said in objection to the doctrine of steadfastness of character may be reaffirmed in the interest of the present one; especially the fact that eternal punishment is a judicially inflicted penalty. If eternal punishment were not

---

does not relieve the matter to refer it to natural law instead of governmental, for God is the author of both. Indeed, it aggravates the difficulty, for there is no reason suggested in the doctrine of natural law for the *eternal* continuance of penalty; no reason why the wicked, for example, should not be annihilated. Still further, God *has* governmental law in this world. He had it in the Jewish theocracy, has it now among Christians— that is, in the laws of the Christian Church—and has it also in the secular world, and has always had it (Rom. xiii). But all of this is and has been based upon natural moral and human relationships.

* The same law which required an atonement in order that God might forgive sin must be the law of necessity in the eternal punishment of those who, in probation, reject that atonement. Both doctrines are one in their philosophy.

a rectoral necessity it would not be represented in the Bible as a penalty inflicted for violation of divine law. Character, we have seen, is unalterably fixed in moral and spiritual ruin when the Holy Ghost forever leaves the soul. In a governmental necessity we find the reason why the Holy Spirit forever takes his flight and leaves the finally impenitent to the natural consequences of moral and spiritual impotency. It is this necessity that fixes the "great gulf" between heaven and hell. God cannot, consistently with justice and the demands of his government, justify the guilty who, in the time of probation, reject the atonement.

It will be needful to ask and answer two questions of difficulty.

1. What is the measure of the intrinsic demerit of sin? It is readily granted that God could not in justice punish sin beyond the measure of its deserts, not even in the interest of moral government. Such *in*justice would be subversive of moral government. Moreover, it is contrary to the character of God. What, then, is the measure of sin's intrinsic demerit? Who, it must be asked, from the very nature of the case, can answer this question but He who alone is omniscient and who possesses the scales of eternal

right? In such a matter it is not for man to presume to answer; it is a fact beyond his reach. If, presumably, God alone is able to answer this question, where shall we find that answer, if it is to be found at all, but in his revealed Word? His Word teaches the fact of eternal punishment. Therefore, we infer that as God is just and his word true, eternal punishment is his revelation to us of the least measure of the intrinsic demerit of sin.

2. The second question relates to the measure of punishment necessary for the conservation of God's moral government. It is not true that God must punish sin to the full extent of its demerit, or to any extent, apart from rectoral considerations.

"Nor has penalty any rational account simply as retributive. It does not so answer to the common moral judgment respecting it, nor to the severe denunciations of Scripture against criminal injuries, nor to the many appeals therein to instances of divine retribution as a deterrent from sin. And for a right exposition of justice we must take large account of its strictly rectoral ends" (Miley, *Atonement in Christ*, p. 222).

This being true, the question recurs, What is the measure of the punishment necessary for the conservation of the divine government? What finite mind, again, shall presume to answer? This, also, is beyond the knowledge of man. We therefore appeal, as before, for our answer to the Scriptures. We there find the same fact of eternal punishment. Therefore, we conclude, as before, that since God is love and would not punish sin beyond the demands of his government even if sin had greater intrinsic demerit, eternal punishment is God's revelation to us of the least measure of punishment necessary for the ends of his government.

Thus we have revealed from heaven the answer to both inquiries. The one fact of eternal punishment revealed, in view of the character of God and the nature of justice, proclaims to us the twofold fact of the eternal demerit of sin and the necessity of an eternal penalty for the ends of divine government.

The following forceful and beautiful statement of truth from Dr. Pope, notwithstanding the criticism offered upon another element of his doctrine, may fitly conclude this discussion:

" The righteousness of divine laws implies also that they are conformed to his aim and purpose, and in this sense right. It is well to believe that they are equal and just in their relation to the creaturely nature. But that is not all. They must be measured by another standard; they are right in their perfect adaptation to the divine plans. Here comes in our apology for the divine Lawgiver: his own supreme theodicy, or vindication of himself. It is not given us to understand the mysteries of the hidden rectoral administration of God. We must believe now that it is righteous; as we shall certainly one day know that it is. *Clouds and darkness are round about him:* unbelief forms out of these clouds, and writes upon this darkness innumerable matters of questioning. But *righteousness and judgment are the habitation of his throne:* behind, all is clear, steadfast, and perfect right. . . . Ten thousand difficulties are swept away, rather are obviated, if we remember that the righteousness of God's moral government is to be measured not only by the creature's nature—it will always bear to be thus measured—but by the design and final end of the economy of his will."

www.ingramcontent.com/pod-product-compliance
Lightning Source LLC
Chambersburg PA
CBHW032007230426
43672CB00010B/2282